CASES in Healthcare Finance

SEVENTH EDITION

CASES in Healthcare Finance

George H. Pink and Paula H. Song

HAP

AUPHA

Health Administration Press, Chicago, Illinois
Association of University Programs in Health Administration, Washington, DC

26 25 24 23 22 5 4 3 2 1

Library of Congress Cataloging-in-Publication Data

Names: Pink, George H., author. | Song, Paula H., author.
Title: Cases in healthcare finance / George H. Pink, Paula H. Song.
Other titles: Gapenski's cases in healthcare finance
Description: Seventh edition. | Chicago, Illinois : Health Administration Press ; Washington, DC : Association of University Programs in Health Administration, [2022] | Preceded by Gapenski's cases in healthcare finance / George H. Pink, Paula H. Song. Sixth edition. 2018. | Summary: "The 33 cases in this book explore financial management and accounting in a variety of healthcare settings. Providing relevant background details, each case presents a financial management decision or challenge for students to analyze and then recommend an appropriate course of action"—Provided by publisher.
Identifiers: LCCN 2021040929 (print) | LCCN 2021040930 (ebook) | ISBN 9781640553170 (paperback ; alk. paper) | ISBN 9781640553149 (epub)
Subjects: MESH: Financial Management, Hospital | Health Care Costs | Health Facilities—economics | Organizational Case Studies | United States
Classification: LCC RA971.3 (print) | LCC RA971.3 (ebook) | NLM WX 157 AA1 | DDC 362.11068/1—dc23
LC record available at https://lccn.loc.gov/2021040929
LC ebook record available at https://lccn.loc.gov/2021040930

The paper used in this publication meets the minimum requirements of American National Standard for Information Sciences—Permanence of Paper for Printed Library Materials, ANSI Z39.48-1984. ♾™

Acquisitions editor: Jennette McClain; Manuscript editor: Jaime Sperling; Project manager: Andrew Baumann; Cover designer: James Slate; Layout: Integra

Found an error or a typo? We want to know! Please e-mail it to hapbooks@ache.org, mentioning the book's title and putting "Book Error" in the subject line.

Health Administration Press
A division of the Foundation of the American College of Healthcare Executives
300 S. Riverside Plaza, Suite 1900
Chicago, IL 60606-6698
(312) 424-2800

Association of University Programs in Health Administration
1730 M Street, NW
Suite 407
Washington, DC 20036
(202) 763-7283

CONTENTS

PREFACE FOR INSTRUCTORS

Healthcare finance can be a fascinating, exciting subject, yet students often regard it as being either too theoretical or too mechanical. The fact is, sound financial decision making requires good theory and analysis plus a great deal of insight and judgment. The best way to get this point across to students, and to demonstrate the inherent richness of the subject, is to relate classroom work to real-world decision making. This way, students must grapple not only with the concepts but also, more important, with how the concepts are applied in practice.

Of course, the most realistic application of healthcare finance occurs within healthcare organizations, and there is no substitute for on-the-job experience. The next best thing, and the only real option for the classroom, is to use cases to simulate the environment in which financial decisions are made.

Purpose

The purpose of this casebook is to provide students with an opportunity to bridge the gap between learning concepts in a classroom setting and applying them in the real world. By using these cases, instructors can help students who have a basic understanding of healthcare finance better prepare for the multitude of problems that arise in practice.

Content

This casebook consists of 33 cases that focus on healthcare finance issues. In general, each finance case addresses a single issue, such as capital budgeting analysis or revenue cycle management, but the uncertainty of the input data, along with the presence of relevant nonfinancial factors, makes each case interesting and challenging. Because the cases focus on both accounting and financial management decisions, they cover the full range of healthcare finance. Furthermore, the cases occur in a wide variety of organizational settings, including hospitals, clinics, medical practices, home health care organizations, integrated delivery systems, and managed care organizations.

Use of the Cases in Courses

The cases can be used in different course formats:

- *Instruction-and-case format.* Some instructors use the cases as assignments in healthcare accounting and financial management courses. A course may include six to seven cases, which the students either present or discuss in class as guided by the instructor.
- *Case-only format.* Some programs with introductory course(s) in accounting and financial management use the cases in a subsequent course to focus on the application of finance concepts within healthcare organizations. This format is essentially a pure case course with 14 to 15 cases (one per week) assigned. The students have had sufficient lecture work in healthcare finance, so at this stage, learning by doing is the best way to prepare them for success in their chosen field.
- *Distance format.* The cases work particularly well in executive MHA programs. Executive students generally bring a great deal of real-world insight into their case analyses, which often makes the discussions livelier than those in traditional programs. In addition, the cases can be worked between class meetings, which allows plenty of time for group discussion and analysis.

Regardless of the course format, cases in healthcare finance are best analyzed by teams as opposed to individual students. Typically, a team of four or five students is assigned to present a case in class. Teams that are not presenting may turn in written reports and act as members of the board of directors during the presentation. They are responsible for asking relevant questions of the presenting team and pointing out any deficiencies in the analysis. Teamwork provides excellent experience for students because almost all decision making in business is done in a group environment, and individuals who cannot work in groups are unlikely to succeed. Students need to know how to motivate the people who work for them and to be able to work with others in a cooperative manner. An in-class presentation also provides students with the opportunity to hone their presentation skills. Healthcare executives constantly state that the ability to communicate is critical to success in business. Knowledge of healthcare finance (or any other managerial discipline) is useless unless people can communicate their ideas to others.

For many instructors, the effective use of this casebook is enhanced by the ancillary materials that are available to those who adopt it:

- Spreadsheet models for students
- Spreadsheet models for instructors
- Case questions
- Case solutions
- PowerPoint presentations

Spreadsheet Models for Students

Spreadsheet analysis has become extremely important in all aspects of healthcare finance, so the cases have accompanying models that allow students to hone and improve their spreadsheet skills. Furthermore, spreadsheet models can reduce the amount of busywork required to perform analyses, giving students more time to focus on the finance issues and qualitative factors that are relevant to the decision at hand.

To facilitate spreadsheet use, we developed well-structured, user-friendly models for each case. The spreadsheet models are efficient and hence big time-savers, especially when conducting risk assessment using techniques such as sensitivity and scenario analyses. In addition, spreadsheet models allow students to easily create graphics and other spreadsheet output that enhance the quality of both the analyses and the presentations.

As we considered students' use of these models, an important question arose: Should we provide complete models to students, or should students be required to do some (or all) of the modeling themselves? After testing several different approaches, we concluded that the best solution for most cases is to provide students with complete versions of the case models such that no modeling is required to obtain a base case solution. However, zeros have been entered for all input data in the student versions, and hence students must identify and then enter the appropriate values. When this is done, the model automatically calculates the base case solution. However, the models do not contain risk analyses or other extensions such as graphics, so students must modify the models as necessary to make them most useful in completing the cases. The student versions of the case models can be accessed through the Health Administration Press website at www.ache.org/books/FinanceCases7. Students should visit the site to download the student versions of the models.

Spreadsheet Models for Instructors

Instructor versions of the spreadsheet models are available for all 33 cases. The instructor models differ from the student models primarily in that the input data are intact in the instructor versions—that is, instructors can view the base case solution without entering any data. In addition, some instructor versions include additional modeling, such as risk analyses.

Case Questions

In general, cases may be classified as directed or nondirected. Directed cases include a specific set of questions that students must answer to complete the case, while nondirected cases (as we use the term) contain only general guidance to point students in the right direction. The primary advantage of nondirected cases is that they closely resemble how real-world managers confront financial decision making, because the cases require students to develop their own solution approach. The disadvantage is that students who stray from the key issues of the cases often do not obtain full value from their effort.

In general, students with more advanced analytical and logic skills and with relevant work experience gain the most from nondirected cases, whereas students who have had less exposure to casework and little or no work experience gain the most from directed cases. The instructor's resources found online for this casebook contain a set of case questions for each case that allow nondirected cases to be converted into directed cases. Thus, instructors have the option of using the cases in either way, depending on the experience of the students, the objectives of the course, and the extent to which cases will be used.

Case Solutions

Each case has a comprehensive solution based on the case questions.

PowerPoint Presentations

Each case is accompanied by a slideshow that introduces the main features of the case and spreadsheet model, presents the solution, and then wraps up the case with three key learning points. Instructors may either use these slides as they are or customize them to meet unique class needs.

Changes in the Seventh Edition

We have used the sixth edition in numerous courses since its publication and have benefited from many student comments and suggestions. Moreover, we have received suggestions from other instructors in a variety of settings. This feedback has resulted in many changes, both substantial and minor.

The cases are ordered and grouped into specific areas of financial management. In addition, they are frequently used in conjunction with the most recent editions of *Healthcare Finance: An Introduction to Accounting and Financial Management (HF)* and *Understanding Healthcare Financial Management (UHFM)*. The cases map to the chapters in these books as shown in the table on page xiv.

Many changes have been made to improve the cases and accompanying materials. Recent changes in the healthcare environment have been incorporated to ensure the cases remain contemporary. Many numerical values have been changed so that revenue and cost figures are more current and so that old case solutions posted on the internet are no longer relevant. Several typos have been corrected, wording and format improvements have been made, and website URLs have been updated.

The most substantial changes to the seventh edition are the following:

- *Case 4: Tulsa Memorial Hospital.* The performance metrics were changed and the data format was revised to increase clarity.
- *Case 6: Big Bend Medical Center.* Substantial revision of case questions and spreadsheets was undertaken to increase clarity.
- *Case 11: Century Oaks Health.* This case is new and focuses on budgeting for a start-up clinic. It asks students to apply revenue

Case	*HF*	*UHFM*
1. New England Healthcare	2	2
2. Beaufort Family Physicians	2	3
3. Santa Fe Healthcare	2	3
4. Tulsa Memorial Hospital	5	
5. Shasta Faculty Practice	5	
6. Big Bend Medical Center	6	
7. Eagan Family Practice	6	
8. Dallas Health Network	6	
9. Cambridge Transplant Center	7	
10. Cascades Mental Health Clinic	8	
11. Century Oaks Health	8	
12. Gulf Shores Surgery Centers	9	4
13. Mid-Atlantic Specialty, Inc.	10	5
14. Pacific Healthcare (A)	11	6
15. Senior Care Enterprises	11	6
16. Pacific Healthcare (B)	12	7
17. Seattle Cancer Center	18	8
18. Southeastern Homecare	13	9
19. RN Temps, Inc.	13	10
20. Jones Memorial Hospital	14	11
21. Coral Bay Hospital	15	12
22. National Rehabilitation Centers	15	12
23. Northwest Suburban Health System	15	12
24. Commonwealth Health Plans	17	13
25. River Community Hospital (A)	17	13
26. River Community Hospital (B)		14
27. Mountain Village Clinic	16	15
28. Foster Pharmaceuticals	16	15
29. Clarinda Community Hospital	16	15
30. Milwaukee Regional Health System	16	15
31. St. Benedict's Teaching Hospital	18	16
32. Beachside Health Partners	18	16
33. Bedford Clinics	18	16

and expense budgeting concepts to a new clinic at both start-up and Year 2.
- *Case 20: Jones Memorial Hospital.* This case was completely rewritten to focus on basic calculations and decision criteria in capital budgeting. The student version of the model is a format guide only because the objective is for students to attempt basic calculations themselves. The key to student success in this case lies in correct calculations and interpretation of the data.

Other substantial changes have been made to the ancillary materials for the seventh edition:

- *Spreadsheet models for students.* All student spreadsheet models have two versions—one set contains tabs with case questions (for the directed case approach), and the other set contains no case questions (for the nondirected case approach). All student spreadsheets are consistent with the instructor spreadsheets. These models have been revised to ensure formula accuracy, to incorporate new Excel functions, and to better present results.
- *Spreadsheet models for instructors.* These models have been revised to ensure formula accuracy, to incorporate new Excel functions, and to better present results.
- *Case questions.* Since the sixth edition, we have gained a lot of in-class experience with the case questions and made modifications to the point that many of the questions included in the seventh edition are completely different from those in the previous edition. We are constantly surprised by the importance of how case questions are worded. For example, a question without "Interpret the results" may lead students to simply submit numerical results without thinking about what they mean. A phrase we have inserted a lot is, "Return to base case assumptions" because students confuse different scenarios. Sometimes, instructors and students themselves have provided us with ideas for new questions that we had not considered before. Our primary goal in making these changes was to improve the pedagogic value of the cases.
- *Case solutions.* Changes to case questions and case data necessitated substantial revision of the case solutions. Sometimes,

changing one number in a spreadsheet entailed changing the entire numerical solution and the way it was written. For example, the discount rates in cases 22 (National Rehabilitation Centers), 23 (Northwest Suburban Health System), 24 (Commonwealth Health Plans), and 26 (River Community Hospital [B]) were changed, which required us to revise the solutions.

- *PowerPoint presentations*. In addition to a list of the main features of the case and three learning points, updated case solutions have been added to the PowerPoint slides. The slides consist of content to be displayed to the class as well as notes to the instructor. Typically, these are 15–20 slides in length and represent the most important improvement to the ancillary materials for this edition.

We are convinced that these changes will make the casebook even more useful for instructors and more beneficial for students in their quest for healthcare finance competency.

Acknowledgments

This casebook reflects the efforts of many people besides the primary authors. First, several of the cases that appear in this and previous editions were coauthored by Murray Côté, Robert Harmon, Ian Jamieson, Brett Justice, and Paul Phillips. In addition, Case 30 (Milwaukee Regional Health System) is coauthored by Scott Hawig, executive vice president of finance at Froedtert Health in Milwaukee, Wisconsin. Finally, colleagues, students, and staff provided inspirational support, as well as more tangible assistance, during the development and class testing of the revised cases. In addition, the Health Administration Press staff was instrumental in ensuring the quality and usefulness of this casebook.

Conclusion

The field of healthcare finance continues to undergo significant changes and advances. Participating in these developments is stimulating, and we sincerely hope that the seventh edition of *Cases in Healthcare Finance* helps students gain a better appreciation for the application of finance principles to healthcare organizations.

A book that raises so many issues will also inevitably generate a variety of opinions regarding both financial theory and practice. Furthermore, although both the publisher and the authors have placed great emphasis on the accuracy of the cases and accompanying materials, some discrepancies or inconsistencies may remain. We appreciate any comments, corrections, criticisms, and ideas for improving all aspects of the cases and related materials.

George H. Pink, PhD
Humana Distinguished Professor
Department of Health Policy and Management
Gillings School of Global Public Health
University of North Carolina at Chapel Hill
1105 McGavran–Greenberg Hall CB 7411
Chapel Hill, NC 27599
E-mail: gpink@email.unc.edu

Paula H. Song, PhD
Richard M. Bracken Chair and Professor
Department of Health Administration
College of Health Professions
Virginia Commonwealth University
Richmond, VA 23284
E-mail: songph@vcu.edu

Instructor Resources

This book's instructor resources, which are fully described in this preface, include instructor versions of the spreadsheet models, case questions, case solutions, and PowerPoint presentations.

For the most up-to-date information about this book and its instructor resources, go to www.ache.org/HAP and search for the book's order code (2450I).

This book's instructor resources are available to instructors who adopt this book for use in their courses. For access information, please e-mail hapbooks@ache.org.

PREFACE FOR STUDENTS

THERE IS NO better way to learn healthcare finance than by working the cases. Of course, first, a basic understanding of the principles and concepts that will be applied in the cases is necessary, and this knowledge is generally obtained from previous classroom work.

The finance cases in this book present situations that require analysis and judgment regarding financial decision making. Although the emphasis here is on financial analysis, real-world decisions are based as much (perhaps more) on qualitative factors as on the numbers. This means you must consider not only the financial implications of the cases but also the relevant nonfinancial factors before reaching final conclusions and making recommendations.

Working the Cases

All cases have accompanying spreadsheet models. These models can be downloaded from the Health Administration Press website at www.ache.org/books/FinanceCases7. Note that the input data in these models have been zeroed out. Thus, you will have to enter the appropriate values for these data to get the models to work. Also, note that the models contain only base case analyses. You must add to the models any extensions required by the case, such as risk analyses and graphics (charts).

Note that for most cases there is more than one right answer. Indeed, in some cases, multiple approaches to the solution may be appropriate. The critical issue in presenting findings is your ability to support your conclusions and recommendations.

An unlimited number of approaches to working the cases exist, and the approach that is optimal for one individual (or group) is not necessarily the best for another individual (or group). That said, here are some suggested steps to help in your casework. (Note that the cases differ in content, and hence one size [the steps below] does not fit all. Also, note that the guidance given here is generic in nature and does not take precedence over the guidance provided by your instructor.)

1. Scan the case to get an overall idea of the setting, topic, and decision at hand.
2. Look at the accompanying spreadsheet model to get a feel for its structure and the nature of the input data needed.
3. Read the case to identify alternative courses of action and to extract the data needed (typically model inputs) for the numerical analysis.
4. Read all the case questions (if provided by the instructor) to get an idea of the types of analyses that will be asked of you.
5. Enter the base case data into the spreadsheet model and check for any problems that might arise, including illogical results.
6. Conduct scenario, sensitivity, and other analyses as needed to either assess risks or make judgments about how uncertainty affects alternative courses of action.
7. Identify the qualitative factors that bear on the decision at hand. Don't forget this step!
8. Reach your final conclusions, which should logically lead to your recommendations.

Most of the information required to successfully work a case is contained in the case itself. However, you may encounter situations in which additional information would allow you either to feel more comfortable in your recommendations or to examine outside-the-box solutions. By all means, feel free to pull data from other sources as needed to create a more complete case solution. In fact, if the data needed are not easily available from other sources, there is nothing wrong with making your own assumptions—as long as they pass the "reasonableness" test.

Making a Presentation

Many of you, either as individuals or as a group, will be required to present your case analysis in class. Generally, your audience will not have written material to refer to (except perhaps supporting financial statements, numerical tables, and so on). Thus, you must structure your presentation so that it can be easily followed and understood the first time around. Although most cases involve a great deal of detailed information, your presentation will be easy to follow if it is simply and clearly organized.

All effective presentations consist of four parts: (1) introduction, (2) body (analysis), (3) conclusions, and (4) recommendations. The first step in preparing a presentation is to construct the body. This is the analysis that must convince the audience that your conclusions and recommendations have merit. If the body is too long and complex, the audience will not be able to grasp its implications and hence will not understand the rationale behind your conclusions and recommendations. Conversely, an analysis that is too short will appear to be lacking in thought and substance and will raise more questions than it will provide answers. Similarly, a body that is not presented in a step-wise, logical sequence may contain the right information but still not get the job done because the audience just can't follow its logic.

Once the body of the presentation has been prepared, the introduction, conclusions, and recommendations should be added. The introduction serves three purposes: (1) to gain the audience's attention, (2) to describe the decision at hand, and (3) to preview the main ideas that will be covered in the remainder of the presentation.

A presentation can have an excellent introduction and body, but it may still be ineffective. There is nothing worse than a presentation that trails off, leaving the audience in the dark as to why they just spent 30 minutes listening to it. The conclusions must be strong and convincing so that the audience recognizes that a sound and thorough analysis has been achieved. Finally, the recommendations must provide concrete suggestions for action. In essence, the conclusions and recommendations should provide closure for the audience. Any questions remaining at this point should involve technical details as opposed to "What did you say we should do?"

Preparing the Slides

Often, you will be using PowerPoint slides as the basis for the presentations. Don't forget that the primary function of slides is to support your message. Thus, the slides must contain the key elements of the introduction, body (analysis), conclusions, and recommendations. Slides that are irrelevant or confusing detract from the presentation. In addition, showing too many slides is just as confusing to the audience as showing too few slides.

Don't put a great deal of numerical detail on the slides. For example, several years of financial statements on a single slide will not be readable. Similarly, breaking the statements into sections so that they are on multiple slides is a poor idea, because the audience will not be able to see all the data at one time. For large amounts of data, handouts are preferable to slides. The key points should be on slides, but use handouts to provide the audience with numerical details.

Final Words

When all is said and done, the key to a good case analysis and presentation is preparedness: "Proper prior planning prevents poor performance." This philosophy applies to all phases of casework, including the presentation itself. How many times have you witnessed a presentation that starts 15 minutes late because the laptop or projector doesn't work or one of the presenters is late? Or, midway through the presentation, a slide either is missing or contains typographical errors? Such small things cast a shadow of doubt over the analysis and presentation—and hence reflect poorly on the entire effort—but they can easily be avoided (and should be) by proper planning.

CASE DESCRIPTIONS

Case 1: New England Healthcare. This case focuses on the development of a premium rate to be offered to a buyer consortium. Students must deal with coverage limitations and copays as well as the basic costs of providing services. In addition, the case requires the conversion of an aggregate per member per month cost into subscriber (single and family) premium rates.

Case 2: Beaufort Family Physicians. This case involves the measurement of physician productivity, financial performance, and quality of care and the use of those measures in determining pay for performance. Alternative methodologies are proposed in the case, and students must choose among the options given. The case also raises issues of how to ensure that compensation systems can be trusted, understood, equitable, and affordable in addition to providing proper incentives.

Case 3: Santa Fe Healthcare. This case focuses on the problems faced by a physician–hospital organization (PHO) when one of its most important payers proposes that its fee-for-service payment methodology change to a fixed per member per month payment. This situation forces the PHO to consider how to handle a full-risk contract that both presents utilization risk and requires the fixed payment and associated risk to be shared among the hospital, specialist physicians, and primary care physicians.

Case 4: Tulsa Memorial Hospital. This case involves the volume break-even analysis of an unprofitable hospital-owned walk-in clinic. Because the spreadsheet model for this case does the busywork, students can concentrate on the problems inherent in volume break-even analysis and its value to managers in making service decisions. In addition, many qualitative factors play a role in this case.

Case 5: Shasta Faculty Practice. This case focuses on the use of advanced practice providers (APPs) in three clinical settings. Students must make judgments about which type of APP (physician assistant or nurse practitioner) is most appropriate for each clinic. In addition, students must perform a cost–benefit analysis to assess the financial impact. The spreadsheet model eases the quantitative burden, but students must make the hard assumptions needed regarding the impact APPs will have on volumes, reimbursements, and costs.

Case 6: Big Bend Medical Center. This case focuses on the question of what constitutes a good cost driver. Students must ponder the fairness of allocating a higher amount of facilities overhead to a department that is being forced to move to a new facility. The case raises many issues regarding cost drivers, fairness, and cost-reduction effectiveness.

Case 7: Eagan Family Practice. This case focuses on the mathematics of cost allocation. Students must use four allocation methods (direct, step-down, double apportionment, and reciprocal) to allocate costs from three support departments to three patient service departments. The case is very mechanical in nature and does not require significant consideration of qualitative issues.

Case 8: Dallas Health Network. This case focuses on using activity-based costing (ABC) techniques to estimate the costs associated with two alternative approaches to providing ultrasound services. Although this case is not complex, it allows students to experience the complexities associated with ABC analysis. The case includes sensitivity analyses on many input variables and considers various qualitative factors that affect the selection decision.

Case 9: Cambridge Transplant Center. This case focuses on the pricing of transplant services. It requires students to do some calculations, but does not involve a large-scale quantitative effort. The primary purpose of the case is to allow students to consider alternative (full vs. marginal) pricing approaches when negotiating with third-party payers. It also emphasizes that, in some situations, marginal costs include marginal fixed costs as well as variable costs.

Case 10: Cascades Mental Health Clinic. This case focuses on a budgeting variance analysis of four managed care product lines. Because of the large number of required calculations, the accompanying spreadsheet model does the mathematical busywork. To add to the mathematical complexity, the case involves both utilization and enrollment differences. Although the calculations are somewhat mechanical, there is ample room for student interpretation and recommendations.

Case 11: Century Oaks Health. This case focuses on budgeting for a start-up clinic. It asks students to apply revenue and expense budgeting concepts to a new clinic at both start-up and Year 2.

Case 12: Gulf Shores Surgery Centers. This case focuses on the mechanics of time value analysis. The case is meant to make students think about the time value process and understand the underlying calculations.

Case 13: Mid-Atlantic Specialty, Inc. This case focuses on basic financial risk concepts. Its goal is to give students a sound understanding of the three types of financial risk (stand-alone, corporate, and market) and their implications for decision making in healthcare organizations.

Case 14: Pacific Healthcare (A). This case focuses on the mechanics of bond valuation as opposed to the managerial decisions inherent in floating a bond issue. Much of the bond valuation work is at the basic level, but the case delves into yield to call and expected rate of return when an issue has a sinking fund.

Case 15: Senior Care Enterprises. This case focuses on the mechanics of the bond refunding decision. The accompanying spreadsheet model does the mathematical busywork. The case presents three refunding options and asks students to make a specific choice. In addition, several qualitative issues are presented.

Case 16: Pacific Healthcare (B). This case takes students through the mechanics of stock valuation (not the managerial decision process that surrounds a new stock issue), including both the constant and nonconstant growth dividend models.

Case 17: Seattle Cancer Center. This case looks at the equipment leasing decisions facing a hospital. The case requires students to perform both lessee's and lessor's analyses. It brings out many side issues, including the correct discount rate, the uncertainty of residual value, the impact of cancellation and per-procedure clauses, and the effects on both parties of leveraging the lease.

Case 18: Southeastern Homecare. This case focuses on the estimation of a business's cost of capital, including both corporate and divisional costs. Because the required calculations are relatively simple, the accompanying spreadsheet model is very basic. However, students must grapple with numerous conceptual issues regarding both estimation methodologies and the interpretation and use of the cost of capital once it is estimated.

Case 19: RN Temps, Inc. This case examines the capital structure decision for an investor-owned company that franchises "rent-a-nurse" businesses. Here, the primary analytical tool is a zero-growth model that calculates stock price under alternative capital structures. However, the case also examines the impact of financial leverage on accounting profits and asks students to consider the business's value under two theoretical models (Modigliani-Miller and Miller). The case also requires students to consider qualitative factors in making the final decision.

Case 20: Jones Memorial Hospital. This case focuses on basic calculations and decision criteria in capital budgeting. The student version of the model is a format guide only because the objective is for students to attempt basic calculations themselves. The key to student success in this case lies in correct calculations and interpretation of the data.

Case 21: Coral Bay Hospital. This case contains a traditional (no nuances) capital budgeting analysis, including cash flow estimation, decision measures, risk assessment, and risk incorporation. In evaluating the financial attractiveness of a proposed outpatient surgery center, students are confronted with many of the problems that occur in such analyses. An accompanying spreadsheet model helps with the calculations. This is a good case for illustrating Monte Carlo simulation.

Case 22: National Rehabilitation Centers. This case focuses on the advantages of making significant capital investments in stages rather than as a large single investment. It uses decision-tree methodology to determine project risk and to illustrate the benefits of abandonment. The accompanying spreadsheet model permits students to spend more time on conceptual matters and takes the tedium out of the calculations.

Case 23: Northwest Suburban Health System. This case investigates three alternative proposals for a hospital system's print shop, including closure and outsourcing all work. It also requires students to grapple with several technical issues related to discounted cash flow analysis, such as the handling of non-normal cash flows. Finally, the case examines the strategic issue of entering the commercial (for-profit) printing market.

Case 24: Commonwealth Health Plans. This case requires the financial statement analysis of a managed care firm. It presents two years of data and discusses benchmarking against primary competitors and the industry.

Case 25: River Community Hospital (A). This case requires the financial statement analysis of a 210-bed hospital, including financial and operating ratio analyses. The accompanying spreadsheet model does most of the calculations, so students can focus on analysis, interpretation, and recommendation for managerial actions.

Case 26: River Community Hospital (B). This case, which builds on the information given in Case 25, focuses on the development of a hospital's forecasted financial statements. It encompasses both forecasting and financial accounting considerations. Although the accompanying spreadsheet model provides a framework for the forecasting process, students must modify the model to incorporate appropriate forecasting techniques. In addition, students must make an extensive set of assumptions about both the future of the hospital industry and the operations of one particular hospital.

Case 27: Mountain Village Clinic. This case is a traditional cash budgeting exercise. It calls for students to develop six monthly budgets, a daily budget for a single month, and a worst-case budget. The spreadsheet model, which reduces the amount of busywork required, facilitates sensitivity analyses regarding both patient volume and collection experience. The case presents students with the opportunity to discuss many facets of cash management.

Case 28: Foster Pharmaceuticals. This case focuses on the basics of receivables management. A start-up drug company is used to illustrate such concepts as average collection period (days sales outstanding), aging schedules, uncollected balances schedules, and the cost of carrying receivables. To complicate matters, these concepts must be applied to multiple customers.

Case 29: Clarinda Community Hospital. This case leads students through an inventory decision process involving supplier selection and optimal ordering quantity (and hence inventory level). The case focuses primarily on the economic ordering quantity model, although students must also categorize inventory items according to the activity-based costing model.

Case 30: Milwaukee Regional Health System. This case focuses on the revenue cycle management process. Students are required to choose appropriate metrics to measure both overall performance and performance within each revenue cycle function. In addition, students must compare both hospital and clinic metric values against national benchmarks and suggest improvement actions where needed. The case also requires students to calculate and compare chargemaster prices to actual reimbursement amounts for several different payers.

Case 31: St. Benedict's Teaching Hospital. This case explores the valuation of a not-for-profit hospital for possible acquisition by another not-for-profit hospital. In addition to the numerical analysis, the case raises several issues related to control after the merger. Although the accompanying spreadsheet model does the busywork, students must think a great deal about the impact of the merger on both entities and future cash flows.

Case 32: Beachside Health Partners. This case focuses on the analysis of a proposed joint venture involving three equity partners: a hospital and group practice as general partners and individual physicians as limited partners. Students must consider both the costs of capital for the partners and the allocation of cash flows to the equity participants. In addition, the case addresses several qualitative issues, including the risks associated with new, unproven technology as well as the ethical and legal issues involved in income-generating referrals.

Case 33: Bedford Clinics. This case requires students to value a family physician group practice. The case provides data to allow students to use both discounted cash flow and market multiple methodologies. Because of a host of qualitative and quantitative issues, the ultimate answer here is filled with uncertainties. The spreadsheet model helps with the calculations.

PART I

THE HEALTHCARE ENVIRONMENT

CASE 1

NEW ENGLAND HEALTHCARE

PREMIUM DEVELOPMENT

New England Healthcare is a regional not-for-profit managed care company headquartered in Hartford, Connecticut. Currently, the company has more than 1 million enrollees in 25 different plans offered in Connecticut, Maine, Massachusetts, New Hampshire, Rhode Island, and Vermont. Recently, a consortium of employers—including major companies such as IBM, GE, and Prudential—contacted New England to bid on a managed care (health maintenance organization) contract the consortium will offer to its 75,000 employees and family members in and around Nashua, New Hampshire.

New England's approach to premium development starts with the recognition that the premium received from employers must cover two different categories of expenses: (1) the cost of providing required healthcare services (medical costs) and (2) the cost of administering the plan and establishing reserves (other costs). Reserves, which are typically required by state insurance regulators, are necessary to ensure that funds are available to pay providers when medical costs exceed the amount collected in premium payments. As a not-for-profit corporation, New England does not explicitly include a profit element in its premium. However, the reserve requirement is set sufficiently high that income from reserve investments is available to fund product expansion and growth; in effect, a portion of the reserve requirement constitutes profit.

New England uses a multistep approach in setting its premiums. First, a base per member per month (PMPM) cost is estimated for each covered benefit of the plan. When the premiums are initially established for a new subscriber group, the base PMPM costs are usually developed on the basis of historical utilization and cost data. If data are available on the specific subscriber group, as with the consortium contract, these data are used. Otherwise, the base PMPM costs are based on utilization and cost data from one or more proxy groups, which are chosen to match as closely as possible the demographic, utilization, and cost patterns that will be experienced under the new contract. In addition, any utilization or cost savings that will result from New England's aggressive utilization management program is factored into the premium.

Second, the base PMPM cost is adjusted to reflect the dollar amount of copayments to providers as well as the estimated impact of copayment and benefit options on utilization and hence medical costs. Copayments, which are an additional source of revenue to the provider panel, reduce New England's medical costs and thus lower the consortium's premium. Furthermore, the higher the copayment, the lower the utilization of that service, especially if it is noncritical.

Finally, limitations are set on the benefits package. The more restrictive the benefits package, the lower the costs associated with medical services. The result of these adjustments is an adjusted PMPM cost for each service. The costs are then summed to obtain the total medical PMPM amount.

To estimate the total nonmedical PMPM amount, New England typically adds 15 percent to the total medical PMPM amount for administrative costs and 5 percent for reserves. The sum of the total medical and total nonmedical amounts—called the *total PMPM amount*—is the per member amount New England must collect each month from the consortium to meet the total costs of serving the healthcare needs of the plan subscribers (the employees).

After the total PMPM amount is calculated, it must be converted into actual premium rates for individual and family coverage. Using data provided by the consortium, New England estimates that 45 percent of subscribers will elect individual coverage, while the remaining 55 percent will choose family coverage. New England plans to offer the consortium a two-rate structure, under which employees may elect either single or family coverage. Data from the consortium indicate that family coverage, on average, includes 3.5 individuals; thus, all else the same, the premiums for family coverage should be 3.5 times as much as for individual coverage. However, children typically consume fewer healthcare services, on a dollar basis, than do adults, so the final premiums must reflect such differentials.

Here are the factor rates for obtaining individual and family premium rates:

Single factor: 1.216	Family factor: 3.356

In setting the specific premium rates, New England must ensure that the total premiums collected, which would be paid by both employer and employees, equal the estimated total calculated using the PMPM rate. The 75,000 members who would be served by the contract consist of roughly 12,000 individuals and 18,000 families. Thus, 75,000 × Total PMPM amount must equal (12,000 × Single premium) + (18,000 × Family premium). **(Note that all the data in this case are for illustrative purposes only and do not reflect current healthcare costs.)**

Exhibit 1.1 is a partially completed copy of the worksheet New England uses to establish the total PMPM amount and the premium rates on any contract. The worksheet is a relatively easy guide for implementing the procedures just described. Exhibit 1.2 contains the relevant cost and utilization adjustment factors for a variety of service and copayment options. Adjustment factors are the decisions made on the appropriate service and copay structure, which feed into the calculations for each service's medical PMPM amount, as shown in exhibit 1.1.

The consortium has furnished New England with a significant amount of data on its employees' current utilization of healthcare services. The employees' inpatient cost and utilization data are as follows:

Average daily fee-for-service charge	$2,800
Utilization ($100 copay)	500 days per year per 1,000 members

Note, however, that a recent survey of New Hampshire hospitals indicates that most managed care contracts call for per diem payments in the range of $2,000 to $2,400. In addition, New England's experience with similar employee groups indicates that moderate utilization management would result in 400 to 450 inpatient days per 1,000 plan members.

Exhibit 1.3 shows the current cost and utilization data for other facility services, including skilled nursing care, inpatient mental health care, hospital surgical services, and emergency department care. The employees' utilization data for primary care services are as follows:

Current number of primary care visits ($5 copay)	3.4 per year per member

New England routinely pays primary care physicians a capitated amount based on an annual cost of $200,000. It assumes that one primary care physician can handle 4,000 patient visits per year. The employees' utilization and cost data for specialist office visits are as follows:

Current number of specialist office visits ($0 copay)	1.5 per year per member
Current cost per visit	$92.65

Note that the total PMPM amount shown in exhibit 1.1 may be modified to reflect anticipated medical cost inflation. This adjustment is especially critical if the total PMPM premium is based on relatively old cost data. The cost data provided in this case can be assumed to be two years old: The data are from the previous year, and the contract would not be in place for yet another year. Also, note that the premium calculation in exhibit 1.1 does not include certain medical services, such as routine vision and dental care, chiropractic services, durable medical equipment, out-of-network services, and pharmacy benefits. The consortium specifically requests that the initial premium bid exclude such "rider" services. However, if New England is chosen to submit a final premium bid, the consortium will likely request pricing on one or more riders.

Finally, with no guidance from the consortium regarding the level of services desired or the copay structure, New England intends to offer three choices to the consortium: low cost, moderate cost, and high cost. The low-cost (to the consortium) plan requires higher copays from employees and has more limitations on covered services. The high-cost plan has lower copays and fewer limitations. The moderate-cost plan falls between the two extremes.

You have recently joined New England Healthcare as its marketing analyst. Your first task is to develop the bid presentation to the consortium.

EXHIBIT 1.1
New England Healthcare: Premium Development Worksheet

I. Medical Expenses

		Copay Adjustment Factors		
	Base PMPM Cost	*Cost*	*Utilization*	*Adjusted PMPM*
Facility Services				
Inpatient:				
Acute	$			$
Skilled nursing				
Mental health				
Substance abuse	0.41	1.0000	1.0000	0.41
Surgical procedures				
Emergency department				
Outpatient procedures	3.43	1.0000	1.0000	3.43
Total facilities				____
Physician Services				
Primary care services				
Specialist services:				
Office visits				
Surgical services	9.00	0.9544	1.0000	8.59
All other services	23.67	0.8659	0.9100	18.65
Total physicians				____
Total medical PMPM amount				____

II. Nonmedical Expenses

Administrative	
Reserves	
Total nonmedical PMPM amount	____

III. Total Expenses

Total PMPM amount

IV. Premium Rates

	Single	*Family*
Rate factor	____	____
Premium rate	____	____

EXHIBIT 1.2
New England Healthcare: Cost and Utilization Adjustment Factors

	Patient Copay Amount	*Copay Cost Adj. Factor*	*Copay Utilization Adj. Factor*
Facility Services			
Inpatient acute	$ 0	1.0000	1.0000
	100	0.9851	0.9750
	150	0.9777	0.9600
	250	0.9642	0.9200
Skilled nursing	$ 0	1.0000	1.0000
Mental health:			
30-day limit	$ 0	1.0000	0.9524
	100	0.9805	0.9286
	150	0.9707	0.9143
	250	0.9532	0.8762
60-day limit	$ 0	1.0000	1.2000
	100	0.9845	1.1700
	150	0.9768	1.1520
	250	0.9628	1.1040
90-day limit	$ 0	1.0000	1.2500
	100	0.9851	1.2188
	150	0.9777	1.2000
	250	0.9643	1.1500
Surgical procedures	$ 0	1.0000	1.0000
	100	0.9231	1.0000
	150	0.8846	1.0000
	250	0.8077	1.0000
Emergency department	$ 0	1.0857	1.0250
	15	1.0000	1.0000
	25	0.9429	0.9850
	50	0.8000	0.9550

EXHIBIT 1.2
New England Healthcare: Cost and Utilization Adjustment Factors (continued)

	Patient Copay Amount	*Copay Cost Adj. Factor*	*Copay Utilization Adj. Factor*
Primary Care Services	$ 0	1.0352	1.0150
	5	1.0000	1.0000
	10	0.9472	0.9800
	15	0.8593	0.9500
	20	0.7713	0.9200
	25	0.6834	0.8900
Specialist Services			
$0 PCP copay	$ 0	1.0000	1.0000
	5	0.8897	0.9730
	10	0.7795	0.9590
	15	0.6692	0.9450
$10 PCP copay	$ 0	1.0000	0.9920
	5	0.8897	0.9600
	10	0.7795	0.9460
	15	0.6692	0.9320
$20 PCP copay	$ 0	1.0000	0.9680
	5	0.8897	0.9360
	10	0.7795	0.9220
	15	0.6692	0.9080

PCP: primary care physician

Note: New England uses various incentive systems to control utilization of specialty services. One system requires PCPs to assess a copay for each specialist office visit.

EXHIBIT 1.3
Consortium Employee Utilization and Cost Data: Other Facility Services

Skilled nursing facility care	25.2 days per year per 1,000 members
Current average daily cost	$650
Inpatient mental health care ($0 copay)	64.4 days per year per 1,000 members
Current average daily cost	$740
Hospital-based surgery ($0 copay)	41.7 cases per year per 1,000 members
Current costs	$1,800 per case
Emergency department care ($15 copay)	132 visits per year per 1,000 members
Current costs	$250 per visit (see note)

Note: The emergency department cost is the total charge for facility services, some of which would be covered by the $15 copay.

CASE 2

BEAUFORT FAMILY PHYSICIANS

PAY FOR PERFORMANCE

Beaufort Family Physicians is a medical group practice located in Beaufort, North Carolina. The practice has four family practice physicians and a medical support staff consisting of a practice manager, two receptionists, four nurses, two medical assistants, two billing clerks, and one laboratory technician. Data relevant to the practice are shown in exhibits 2.1 through 2.3.

Beaufort is organized as a partnership, with each physician having an equal share. Although the practice manager has the authority to make the day-to-day business decisions, all strategic decisions are made jointly by the partners. In addition, Beaufort uses a local certified public accountant (CPA) to prepare and file its taxes and to act as a financial adviser when needed.

At Beaufort, the current policy is to provide equal compensation to all four physicians. Last year, each physician was paid the same monthly salary ($14,167). At the end of the year, profits that were not needed for reinvestment in new assets were divided equally among the partners ($30,000 each). Although this "equal pay for equal work" policy has been in place since Beaufort was founded in 1996, it has caused growing discontent among the partners. Not surprisingly, each of the physicians believes that they work harder than the others and hence should receive greater compensation. In addition, the physicians recognize the importance of putting away some profits to pay for new medical equipment that will replace aging items and to expand the range of services offered.

A recent survey by the Medical Group Management Association indicated that less than 10 percent of group practice family physicians are compensated on a straight salary basis, while the majority are compensated on the basis of productivity. Of those compensated according to productivity measures, about half are paid solely on productivity and half receive a base salary plus a bonus component based either on productivity alone or on productivity and other measures. (For more information on the Medical Group Management Association, see www.mgma.com.)

To reward those physicians who truly work harder and to create the incentive for all physicians to be as productive as possible, the partners instructed the practice manager to assess the current compensation system and to recommend any changes that would improve the system.

You are the practice manager at Beaufort Family Physicians. As a start, you scheduled a meeting with the partners to gain some initial guidance. At this meeting, the partners agreed that any proposed system must have the following five characteristics:

1. *The system must be trusted.* Physicians must trust not only the data used but also the integrity and competency of the individuals who administer the system. The compensation model itself may be sound, but a lack of faith in either the data or the administration of the system will lead to a lack of confidence in the entire system.
2. *The system must be clearly understood.* In the search for the perfect system, practice managers tend to create a model that is overly complex, and hence the links between pay and performance cannot be easily identified. If the physicians cannot easily identify what performance is necessary to increase pay, the system will not have the desired results.
3. *The system must be perceived to be equitable.* If the physicians do not believe that the system is fair—that is, those physicians who contribute more are paid more—it is doomed to fail.
4. *The system must create the proper incentives.* A fundamental objective of any compensation plan is to maintain the financial viability of the organization. Thus, the model must create incentives that promote behavior that contributes to the success of the group. Furthermore, the incentives offered must be large enough to encourage the physicians to change their behavior.
5. *The system must be affordable.* The costs of implementing and administering the system must be reasonable. Furthermore, the total amount of incentive compensation paid must not impair the ability of the practice to cover its operating costs, replace existing assets, or acquire new assets.

The general agreement among the physicians is that the compensation system should consist of a base salary plus some form of pay-for-performance scheme. For example, each physician might receive a base salary of $6,000 per month, and the remaining compensation would be based on some measure(s) of performance.

Even with this agreement, the task of making recommendations for change in the physician compensation system is daunting. After all, many systems are available, each with its own strengths and weaknesses. To gain a better appreciation of the possible choices, you downloaded from the internet several articles about pay for performance. Then, you met with Jennifer Wong, Beaufort's CPA, to learn about alternative systems used at other practices. After several meetings with Jennifer, you conclude that the following potential measures might be appropriate for Beaufort's pay-for-performance plan.

Productivity Measures

- *Number of patient visits.* This measure is a simple count of the annual number of patient visits for a physician, regardless of the time per visit or type of patient. More patient visits indicate higher physician productivity.
- *Work relative value units (RVUs).* Jennifer consulted with another group practice that uses RVUs to measure productivity. RVUs form the basis of physician compensation for Medicare services. Under this system, each physician service has three relative value components: (1) physician work, (2) practice expense, and (3) malpractice expense. More work RVUs indicate higher productivity.
- *Professional procedures.* This measure is a simple count of the annual number of procedure codes (such as injections), regardless of the time per procedure, type of procedure, or reimbursement amount. More professional procedures indicate higher productivity.

Financial Measures

- *Gross charges.* This measure is the total gross charges generated by a physician during the year (discounts, allowances, and costs are ignored). Gross charges are easily identified from the current billing system used by the practice. More gross charges indicate higher physician financial performance.

- *Net collections.* This measure is the total collected revenue generated by a physician during the year (gross charges minus discounts and allowances; again, costs are ignored). Net collections are also easily identified from the current billing system used by Beaufort. Greater net collections indicate higher financial performance.
- *Net income.* This measure is the total net income (before physician compensation) generated by a physician during the year. As stated, gross charges and net collections are easily identified from the current billing system used by Beaufort. However, this measure requires allocation of practice costs to individual physicians. With limited data at hand, one possible solution is to divide the total costs of the practice into fixed and variable components and then allocate the fixed component equally to all four physicians and allocate the variable component on the basis of some measure of resource utilization, such as professional procedures. Higher net income indicates higher financial performance.

Quality Measures

- *Average patient satisfaction.* This measure is an average of the patient satisfaction scores for a physician. Higher patient satisfaction scores indicate higher physician quality.
- *Blood pressure control.* This measure indicates whether a physician met a target for blood pressure control among the patients seen during the year. The Centers for Medicare & Medicaid Services (CMS) sponsors the Merit-Based Incentive Payment System (MIPS) under its Quality Payment Programs. Participating physicians in MIPS are eligible to earn payment increases if they meet performance targets on a variety of quality measures. Blood pressure control is one of the quality measures that apply to all Medicare beneficiaries who meet age and sex criteria. Attaining the target indicates higher quality.
- *Breast cancer screening.* This is another MIPS quality measure that applies to all Medicare beneficiaries who meet age and sex criteria. Attaining the target indicates higher quality.

Of course, any combination of these measures could be used, making a wide variety of solutions possible.

Armed with this information, you held another meeting with the partners and Jennifer to understand their views regarding physician compensation. The meeting had three agenda items: (1) Should pay for performance be based on productivity, financial performance, and/or quality? (2) What total dollar amount should be allocated to performance pay versus base salary? (3) What amount of net income (after physician compensation) should the practice target?

At the beginning of the meeting, all agreed that the physicians who contribute most to Beaufort should receive the highest compensation. However, they could not reach an agreement on how to define "contribute most." For example, one physician stated that work effort is the most meaningful measure. "Let's just use the number of patient visits—it's simple, and we all agree that more visits require more work," he argued. But this was challenged by another physician, who stated that many of her patients are elderly and chronically ill and require much more time per visit than do younger, healthier patients. Work RVUs are another basis of measuring productivity, but the physicians weren't sure about using the data from a billing system for such a purpose. Another physician argued that the real money is in procedures. Historically, physicians have been paid relatively well for diagnostic and treatment procedures, and group practices that do a lot of procedures have done well financially. Therefore, it makes sense to reward those physicians who perform higher numbers of professional procedures. But another physician was uncomfortable with rewarding such a narrow part of clinical practice. "Besides," he said, "I am getting older and don't do as many procedures as I once did."

Next, the discussion turned to financial performance measures. Although one physician strongly believed that gross charges were the best measure, another countered that (1) gross charges do not reflect reimbursement amounts and (2) gross charges generated at the expense of high costs do not financially help the practice much. Jennifer jumped in at that point, saying that the strength of the net income measure is that physicians are held responsible for both revenues and costs. Thus, physicians would have the incentive to be more productive (generate more revenues) while reducing the costs associated with operating the practice. However, the cost allocation required for calculation of net income can only be roughly estimated, so it will be difficult to convince the physicians that the allocation has true economic meaning.

Performance pay based on quality was the last item discussed. One physician stated that too much emphasis is placed on money. If the physicians do not provide high-quality medical care and keep their patients happy, there will be no patients and hence no revenues. Thus, she argued, "Patient satisfaction is just as important as revenue generation." In addition to the patient satisfaction issue, one partner noted that Beaufort physicians provide care to many Medicare beneficiaries. "It's important to gain experience with the Quality Payment Program that CMS implemented," he argued. However, the reaction to this comment was mixed. Two partners thought the whole idea of rewarding physicians for practicing good medicine was ludicrous. One commented that the profession is in a sad state of affairs if physicians have to be paid extra to do what is right. On the other hand, another partner stated that if this was the trend among payers, it might be wise to build similar quality guidelines into Beaufort's compensation system.

At the end of the discussion on agenda item 1, one physician stated, "It's clear we don't agree on how to measure performance, so why don't we just use all the measures? Then everybody will be happy." The thought of using all of the measures made you shudder because of the complexity of interpreting the results and the administrative burden that would be required.

Then, the meeting turned to agenda item 2: the actual amount to be allocated to performance pay. One physician suggested that, because they could not agree on how to measure performance, compensation should be composed mostly of base salary and only a small amount of performance pay—say, $10,000 per physician. This brought a chorus of "Why bother?" from the other physicians. "This isn't enough of an incentive for anything—after all, we spend more than that on lattes," one joked. In contrast, another physician stated, "I'd prefer to base all our compensation on performance. Who can argue with productivity, financial performance, and quality?" After a prolonged discussion, the only agreement reached was that the dollar amount allocated to performance pay should be high enough to make physicians pay attention to performance but should be less than the amount of base salary.

Agenda item 3 revolved around the target net income (after physician compensation). In contrast to their dissension on the other agenda items, all the physicians readily agreed that the net income after physician compensation of the practice has to be at least $70,000 to pay for new medical equipment that the practice requires.

At the end of the meeting, you could tell that the task of revising Beaufort's compensation system would not be easy. None of the approaches initially identified could be ruled out. Furthermore, you are given only broad direction on the dollar amount to be allocated for performance pay. Your major hurdle is to develop a system that would be supported by all four partners. Thus, the ability to "sell" the system to the partners is just as important as the system itself.

To ensure an orderly approach to the assignment, you decide to (1) use the historical allocation between base salary and performance pay as a starting point, (2) assess the sensitivity of physician pay to the various performance measures, and (3) recommend the system you believe is best for Beaufort. Finally, you recognize that the merits of alternative compensation systems are influenced somewhat by the nature of the practice's revenue stream (reimbursement). Almost half of Beaufort's revenues come from Medicare and Medicaid, and the remainder comes from commercial insurers, including managed care plans. Some of the managed care plans were using capitated payment systems several years ago, but today, all of Beaufort's payers use fee-for-service methodologies.

EXHIBIT 2.1
Beaufort Family Physicians: Historical Support Staff Salaries

	Number of Employees	*Total Compensation*
Practice manager	1	$ 79,168
Receptionists	2	48,652
Nurses	4	248,000
Medical assistants	2	53,615
Billing clerks	2	64,165
Laboratory technician	1	46,788
Total		$540,388

EXHIBIT 2.2
Beaufort Family Physicians: Historical Financial Data

Gross charges	$2,320,648
Net collections	$1,845,059
Practice expenses:	
Support staff salaries	$ 540,388
Facilities cost	298,351
Supplies cost	136,257
Total practice expenses	$ 974,996
Net income before physician compensation	$ 870,063
Physician compensation:	
Base salaries	$ 680,000
Bonus	120,000
Total physician compensation	$ 800,000
Net income after physician compensation	$ 70,063

EXHIBIT 2.3
Beaufort Family Physicians: Historical Physician Data

	Physician Identifier				
	A	*B*	*C*	*D*	*Total*
Patient visits	4,023	3,567	3,966	4,244	15,800
Number of RVUs	4,667	5,055	5,475	4,967	20,164
Professional procedures	6,255	6,972	7,287	6,742	27,256
Gross charges	$547,820	$560,841	$625,675	$586,312	$2,320,648
Net collections	$442,256	$439,881	$441,872	$521,050	$1,845,059
Average patient satisfaction score	89	80	87	94	
Blood pressure control target met?	Yes	Yes	Yes	No	
Breast cancer screening target met?	No	Yes	No	No	

RVUs: relative value units

Notes: 1. The RVUs listed are work RVUs, which are only one of the three components used in Medicare physician reimbursement.
2. Over the past five years, the average annual amount reinvested in the practice was $70,000.
3. Patient satisfaction scores are measured using a 100-point scale.

CASE 3

SANTA FE HEALTHCARE

CAPITATION AND RISK SHARING

Santa Fe Memorial Hospital is a community hospital in Green Bay, Wisconsin. Recently, the hospital and its affiliated physicians formed Santa Fe Healthcare, a physician–hospital organization (PHO). Santa Fe is close to signing its first contract to provide exclusive local healthcare services to enrollees in BadgerCare (the Plan), the local Blue Cross Blue Shield of Wisconsin HMO. For the past several years, the Plan has contracted with a different Green Bay PHO, but financial difficulties at that organization have prompted the Plan to consider Santa Fe as an alternative. In the proposed contract, Santa Fe will assume full risk for patient utilization. In fact, the proposal calls for Santa Fe to receive a fixed premium of $200 per member per month from the Plan, which it can then allocate to each provider component in any way it deems best using any reimbursement method it chooses.

Santa Fe's executive director, Dr. George O'Donnell, a cardiologist and recent graduate of the University of Wisconsin Nonresident Program in Administrative Medicine, is evaluating the Plan's proposal. To help do this, Dr. O'Donnell hired a consulting firm that specializes in PHO contracting.

The first task of the consulting firm was to review Santa Fe's current medical panel and estimate the number of physicians, by specialty, required to support the Plan's patient population of 50,000, assuming aggressive utilization management. The results in exhibit 3.1 show that Santa Fe's medical panel currently consists of 249 physicians, whereas the number of physicians required to support the Plan's patient population is only 59. Note, however, that Santa Fe physicians serve patients other than those in the Plan. Thus, the total number of physicians required to treat all of Santa Fe's patients far exceeds the 59 shown in the right column of exhibit 3.1.

The second task of the consulting firm was to analyze Santa Fe physicians' current practice patterns. Clearly utilization, and hence cost, is driven by Santa Fe's physicians, and variation in practice patterns is costly to Santa Fe. Results of the analysis show significant variation in practice patterns, both in the physicians' offices and in the hospital. For example, exhibit 3.2 contains summary data on hospital costs by physician for three common Medicare Severity Diagnosis Related Groups (MS-DRGs). Consider MS-DRG 470 (major joint replacement). The physician with the lowest hospital costs averaged $12,872 in costs per patient, the highest-cost physician averaged $24,638, and the average cost for all physicians was $14,999. The consulting firm commented that reducing this variation is important because Santa Fe is at full risk for patient utilization.

The third task of the consulting firm was to recommend an appropriate allocation of the premium dollars to each category of provider. Specifically, the contract calls for Santa Fe to receive $200 per member per month, for a total annual revenue of $200 × 50,000 members × 12 months = $120 million. To reduce potential conflicts about how to divide the $120 million among providers, the consulting firm proposed a "status quo" allocation that would maintain the current revenue distribution percentages shown in exhibit 3.3.

The final task of the consulting firm was to recommend provider reimbursement methodologies that create appropriate incentives. In the contract, Santa Fe assumes full risk for patient utilization, so the consulting firm recommended that all component providers be capitated to align cost minimization incentives throughout Santa Fe. Furthermore, capitation of all providers would eliminate the need for risk pools, a risk-sharing arrangement that Santa Fe has never used. In addition to the consulting firm's report, Dr. O'Donnell decided to ask Santa Fe's new operations committee for a short report on the current line of thinking among Santa Fe's major providers. The committee provided the following information.

Santa Fe Memorial Hospital

Historically, the profitability of Santa Fe Memorial Hospital has been roughly in line with the industry. Last year, when the hospital received about 75 percent of charges, on average, it achieved an operating margin of about 3 percent. However, hospital managers are concerned about its profitability if the Plan's proposal is accepted. The managers believe that controlling costs under the full-risk contract would require extraordinary efforts and that the most effective way to control costs is to create a subpanel of physicians to participate in the capitation contract. When asked how the subpanel should be chosen, the operations committee recommended choosing the physicians who would do the best job of containing hospital costs.

Primary Care Physicians

Many of the primary care physicians are dissatisfied. On average, primary care physicians receive only about 60 percent of charges and are concerned about being penalized by accepting utilization risk for the Plan's enrollees. Primary care physicians know that they are paid less and believe that they have to work much harder than the specialists. Furthermore, primary care physicians believe that the specialists supplement their own incomes by overusing in-office tests and procedures. Some primary care physicians are even talking about dropping out of Santa Fe to form their own contracting group, taking away the entire capitation payment from the Plan and contracting themselves for specialist and hospital services.

Specialist Care Physicians

The specialists believe that the primary care physicians refer too many patients to them. The specialists do not mind the referrals as long as their reimbursement is based on charges because, on average, they receive 90 percent of charges. However, if they are capitated, the specialists want the primary care physicians to handle more of the minor patient problems themselves. Also, whenever the subject of subpanels is raised, many of the specialists become incensed. "After all," they say, "the whole idea behind the PHO is to protect the specialists." Both sets of physicians—primary care and specialist—agree that the hospital is hopelessly inefficient. Said one specialist, "No matter how much revenue the hospital receives, it still seems to barely make a profit."

To respond to the Plan's proposal, Dr. O'Donnell and Santa Fe's executive committee must decide whether to accept the recommendations of the consulting firm.

You have been hired to advise Dr. O'Donnell and the executive committee regarding these challenges. Because your report will serve as the basis of Santa Fe's implementation plan if it accepts BadgerCare's contract, the report must address the concerns raised by the physicians and the hospital. Furthermore, the report must include specific recommendations on how to implement these changes.

EXHIBIT 3.1
Santa Fe Healthcare: Physician PHO Members and Estimated Needs for 50,000 Enrollees

Specialty	*Number in PHO*	*Estimated Need per 50,000 Enrollees*
General medicine	42	20.9
Pediatrics	15	4.1
Total primary care	57	25.0
Anesthesiology	9	2.5
Cardiology	12	1.4
Emergency medicine	10	2.5
General surgery	13	2.7
Neurosurgery	3	0.3
Obstetrics/gynecology	27	5.4
Orthopedics	11	2.5
Psychiatry	19	1.9
Radiology	8	3.0
Thoracic surgery	0	0.4
Urology	5	1.3
Other specialties	75	10.1
Total specialists	192	34.0
Grand total	249	59.0

EXHIBIT 3.2
Hospital Costs for Three Common MS-DRGs by Physician

MS-DRG	*Description*	*Minimum*	*Average*	*Maximum*
470	Major joint replacement or reattachment of lower extremity without MCC	$12,872	$14,999	$24,638
871	Septicemia or severe sepsis without MV; 96+ hours with MCC	4,271	13,729	17,394
291	Heart failure and shock with MCC	6,498	10,849	18,015

MCC: major complication or comorbidity; MV: mechanical ventilation.
Note: This exhibit is based on historical costs related to the severity-adjusted Medicare Severity Diagnosis Related Groups (MS-DRGs).

EXHIBIT 3.3
Santa Fe Healthcare: Proposed Allocation of Premium Dollars

PHO administration/overhead	13%
Paid to in-system physicians	
Primary care	10
Specialists	18
Ancillary services	5
Administration/profit	1
Paid to in-system hospital	38
Paid for prescription drugs	10
Paid to out-of-system providers	5
Total premium dollar	100%

PART II

COST BEHAVIOR AND PROFIT ANALYSIS

CASE 4

TULSA MEMORIAL HOSPITAL

BREAK-EVEN ANALYSIS

Tulsa Memorial Hospital (TMH), an acute care hospital with 300 beds and 160 staff physicians, is one of 75 hospitals owned and operated by Health Services of America, a for-profit, publicly owned company. Nine other acute care hospitals serve the same general population, but Tulsa historically has been highly profitable because of its well-appointed facilities, its fine medical staff, its reputation for quality care, and the amount of individual attention it gives to its patients. In addition, Tulsa operates an emergency department (ED) within the hospital complex and a stand-alone urgent care center located across the street from the area's major shopping mall, about two miles from the hospital.

According to a *Wall Street Journal* article, urgent care centers are increasingly visited by patients who need immediate treatment for an illness, such as the flu or a sore throat, or an injury, such as a nail-gun wound. Urgent care centers are distinguished from similar types of ambulatory healthcare providers, such as EDs and retail clinics, by the scope of illnesses treated and the presence of on-site facilities. These centers help mitigate the problems of primary care physician shortages and already crowded (and typically very expensive) EDs. Urgent care centers, notes the *Wall Street Journal* article, are staffed by physicians, offer short wait times, and charge between $60 and $200 per procedure. Furthermore, no appointments are necessary, and evening and weekend hours are frequently available. Finally, many centers offer discounts to the uninsured, and for those with coverage, copayments are typically much less than for ED visits. Currently, about 9,000 urgent care centers are in operation across the United States, including about 1,500 that are hospital affiliated.

The Urgent Care Association of America has established criteria for designation as a certified urgent care center. Currently, about half the centers in the United States have this certification. According to MedLibrary.org, "these criteria define scope of service, hours of operation, and staffing requirements. A qualifying facility must accept walk-in patients of all ages during all hours of operation. It should treat a 'broad-spectrum' of illnesses and injuries, and have the ability to perform minor procedures. An urgent care center must also have on-site diagnostic services, including phlebotomy and x-ray." (For more information on urgent care centers, see www.ucaoa.org.) In addition, urgent care centers can obtain accreditation through The Joint Commission as part of its ambulatory healthcare accreditation program. (For more information, see www.jointcommission.org.)

Brandon Harley, Tulsa's CEO, is concerned about the urgent care center's overall financial soundness. About 10 years ago, several area hospitals jumped onto the urgent care center bandwagon, and within a short time, 15 such centers were scattered around the city. Now, only 11 are left, and none of them appears to be a big moneymaker. Brandon wonders if Tulsa should continue to operate its urgent care center or close it. The urgent care center currently handles a patient load of 45 visits per day, but it has the physical capacity to handle up to 85 visits a day. Brandon's decision is complicated by the fact that Amanda Daniels, Tulsa's marketing director, has been pushing to expand the marketing program for the urgent care center. She believes that an expanded marketing effort aimed at local businesses would bring in the number of new patients needed to make the urgent care center a financial winner.

Brandon has asked Nicole Williams, Tulsa's chief financial officer, to analyze the options. In their meeting, Brandon stated that he visualizes three potential outcomes for the urgent care center: (1) close it, (2) continue to operate it without expanding marketing, or (3) continue to operate it with an expanded marketing effort. As a starting point, Nicole collected the most recent historical financial and operating data for the urgent care center, which are summarized in exhibit 4.1. In assessing the historical data, she noted that one competing center had recently (December 2019) closed its doors. Furthermore, a review of several years of financial data revealed that the urgent care center does not have a pronounced seasonal utilization pattern.

Next, Nicole met several times with the urgent care center's administrative director. The primary purpose of the meetings was to estimate the additional costs that would have to be borne if volume rose above the current January/February average level of 45 visits per day. Any incremental usage would require additional expenditures for administrative and medical supplies: estimated to be $5 per patient visit for medical supplies, such as tongue blades and rubber gloves, and $2 per patient visit for administrative supplies, such as file folders and clinical record sheets.

Because of the relatively low volume level, the urgent care center has purposely been staffed at the bare minimum. In fact, some employees have started to grumble about not being able to do their jobs well because of overwork. Thus, any increase in the number of patient visits would require immediate administrative and medical staffing increases. The incremental costs associated with increased volume are summarized in exhibit 4.2.

The urgent care center's building is leased on a long-term basis. Tulsa could cancel the lease, but the lease contract calls for a cancellation penalty of three months' rent, or $37,500 at the current rate. In addition, Nicole was startled to read in the newspaper that Baptist Hospital, Tulsa's major competitor, had just bought the city's largest primary care practice, and Baptist's CEO was quoted as saying that more group practice acquisitions are planned as the hospital moves to embrace healthcare reform. Nicole wondered whether Baptist's actions would influence the decision regarding the urgent care center's fate.

Finally, Nicole met with Amanda to learn more about the proposed marketing expansion. The primary focus of the expansion would be on occupational health services (OHS). OHS involves providing medical care to employees of local businesses, including physical examinations; treatment of illnesses that occur during working hours; and treatment of work-related injuries, especially those covered by workers' compensation. Some of the urgent care center's business is already OHS related, but Amanda believes that a strong marketing effort, coupled with specialized OHS record keeping, could bring additional patients to the urgent care center. The proposed marketing expansion requires a marketing assistant who will run the effort for the OHS program. In addition, marketing would incur advertising costs for newspaper, radio, and TV ads as well as for brochures and handouts. The incremental costs associated with marketing are also summarized in exhibit 4.2. (To learn more about OHS, start at the American College of Occupational and Environmental Medicine website, www.acoem.org.)

With a blank spreadsheet on her computer screen, Nicole began to construct a model that shows the information the board needs to make a rational, financially sound decision. At first, Nicole planned to conduct a standard capital budgeting analysis that focused on the profitability of the urgent care center as measured by net present value or internal rate of return. But she realized that expanded marketing requires no capital investment and no valid data are available on the incremental increase in visits that would be generated by either an increasing population base or the expanded marketing. Finally, she remembered that Brandon requested that the analysis consider the inherent profitability of the urgent care center without the expanded marketing effort.

With these points in mind, Nicole thought that a break-even analysis would be useful in making the final decision. Specifically, she wanted to develop answers to the following questions posed by Brandon:

- What is the projected profitability of the urgent care center for the entire year if volume continues at its current level?
- How many additional visits per day would be required to break even without the expanded marketing?
- How many additional visits per day would be required to break even, assuming that marketing is expanded?
- How many additional daily visits would expanded marketing have to bring in to make it worthwhile, regardless of the overall profitability of the urgent care center?

In addition, Nicole wondered if the urgent care center could "inflate" its way to profitability; that is, if volume remained at its current level, could the urgent care center be expected to become profitable in, say, five years, solely because of inflationary increases in revenues? Finally, Nicole was concerned about whether the analysis was giving the urgent care center full credit for its financial contributions to Tulsa. She did not want to change the spreadsheet at this late date, but she did want to make sure that any additional financial value was at least considered qualitatively. Overall, Nicole must consider all relevant factors—both quantitative and qualitative—and come up with a recommendation regarding the future of the urgent care center.

EXHIBIT 4.1
TMH Urgent Care Center: Historical Financial Data

	Current Year			*Monthly Averages*		
	2021	*Jan 2022*	*Feb 2022*	*2021*	*Jan/Feb 2022*	*Total*
Number of visits	14,522	1,365	1,335	1,210	1,350	1,230
Net revenue	$548,747	$55,028	$54,748	$45,729	$54,888	$47,037
Salaries and wages	$154,250	$13,540	$13,544	$12,854	$13,542	$12,952
Physician fees	192,000	18,000	18,000	16,000	18,000	16,286
Malpractice insurance	31,440	3,215	3,215	2,620	3,215	2,705
Travel and education	5,365	538	665	447	602	469
General insurance	8,112	843	843	676	843	700
Subscriptions	189	0	0	16	0	14
Electricity	11,820	1,124	1,029	985	1,077	998
Water	1,260	135	142	105	139	110
Equipment rental	1,260	105	105	105	105	105
Building lease	155,745	12,500	12,500	12,979	12,500	12,910
Other operating expenses	103,779	8,152	7,923	8,648	8,038	8,561
Total operating expenses	$665,220	$58,152	$57,966	$55,435	$58,059	$55,810
Operating income (loss)	($116,473)	($ 3,124)	($ 3,218)	($ 9,706)	($ 3,173)	($ 8,773)
Gross margin	(21.2%)	(5.7%)	(5.9%)	(21.2%)	(5.8%)	(18.7%)

EXHIBIT 4.2
TMH Urgent Care Center: Monthly Incremental Cost Data

	Number of Additional Visits per Day				
	0	*1–10*	*11–20*	*21–30*	*31–40*
Variable Costs					
Medical supplies			$5 per visit		
Administrative supplies			2 per visit		
Total variable costs per visit			$7 per visit		
Semifixed Costs					
Salaries and wages		$ 5,000	$ 6,000	$ 7,000	$ 8,000
Physician fees		12,000	12,000	12,000	16,000
Total monthly semifixed costs	$ 0	$ 17,000	$18,000	$19,000	$24,000
Fixed Costs					
Marketing assistant's salary	$ 3,000	$ 3,000	$ 3,000	$ 3,000	$ 3,000
Advertising expenses	4,000	4,000	4,000	4,000	4,000
Total monthly fixed costs	$ 7,000	$ 7,000	$ 7,000	$ 7,000	$ 7,000

CASE 5

SHASTA FACULTY PRACTICE

COST—BENEFIT ANALYSIS

SHASTA FACULTY PRACTICE (the Practice) is the not-for-profit corporation that controls the clinical operations of the medical faculty of Shasta University. The Practice provides all physician services for Shasta Health System (the System), which consists of five hospitals plus supporting services that, together, provide the entire continuum of care. The main inpatient facility is a 650-bed tertiary care academic medical center, although the System also owns two rural 50-bed hospitals, a 125-bed community hospital, and an 80-bed long-term care facility. In addition, the System owns multiple outpatient clinics and has established joint ventures with several other outpatient providers.

The Practice's vice president for outpatient services, Dr. Ruby Kim, is exploring the use of advanced practice providers (APPs) such as nurse practitioners (NPs) and physician assistants (PAs) in the clinics to enhance physician productivity and, ultimately, the Practice's profitability. The roles of APPs have evolved to the point where they can perform more than 80 percent of primary care physicians' patient care duties. They take medical histories, perform physical examinations, diagnose and treat illnesses, order and interpret laboratory tests, and, in most situations, prescribe medications. Historically, NPs (along with other advanced practice nurses) and PAs were referred to as *physician extenders*, *mid-level providers*, or *nonphysician providers*; however, these terms do not accurately reflect the full scope of practice and expertise of APPs. For example, NPs and PAs are licensed, independent practitioners who work at the top of their license. They are part of a patient care team that includes physicians and other clinicians.

The use of APPs allows physicians to treat more and higher-acuity patients, expediting patient flow and increasing revenues. In addition, because compensation for APPs is less than that for physicians, costs per patient visit can be lowered. Aside from the obvious productivity and economic benefits, studies indicate that patient satisfaction improves when APPs are used. APPs are often able to spend more time with each patient than physicians usually do. This extra attention typically results in higher patient satisfaction without diminishing quality of care.

As the role of APPs expanded, it was inevitable that some conflicts would arise. The increasing recognition by third-party payers that, for example, NPs are as qualified as physicians to provide many services means these advanced practice professionals are a potential source of direct competition for physicians. Still, physicians at many solo and group practices are using APPs to support and complement their work. Adding to the APP trend, predicted shortages of 21,400–55,000 primary care physicians by 2033 (according to the Association of American Medical Colleges) mean that APPs will play an important role in filling the physician void to prevent reduced access to primary care.

The two main types of APPs are NPs and PAs. Although NPs and PAs often perform similar tasks, their training and certification requirements differ. NPs must be licensed in the state in which they practice. To acquire such licensure, an individual must be licensed as a registered nurse, meet additional education and practicum requirements that historically led to a master's degree, and pass a national certification examination in one of several specialized areas. Now, however, most nursing schools that offer nurse practitioner education are transitioning to programs that lead to doctor of nursing practice (DNP) degrees. This trend has created an expectation that, at some future date, the DNP degree will become a requirement for certification. (For more information on NPs, see the website of the American Association of Nurse Practitioners at www.aanp.org.)

PAs must graduate from an accredited physician assistant educational program and then obtain certification by the National Commission on Certification of Physician Assistants. The educational training for a PA is similar to that of a physician but is much shorter—historically only two years. PA programs traditionally offered either associate or bachelor's degrees, but most programs today are at the master's level. (For more information on PAs, see the website of the American Academy of Physician Assistants at www.aapa.org.)

Although it may appear that NPs and PAs are perfect substitutes for one another, the differences in educational background create differences in philosophies of care. Because NPs follow the nursing model of care, which focuses on health education and counseling as well as disease prevention, they typically have a special concern for the overall health and welfare of patients. PAs, on the other hand, generally follow the medical model of care, which focuses on diagnosis and treatment. Of course, these are generalizations that do not necessarily apply to specific individuals. Although most NPs and PAs practice in primary care settings, others specialize in such areas as dermatology, pediatrics, geriatrics, anesthesiology, surgery, and emergency medicine.

The practice status of APPs has been, in large part, driven by state law. Historically, some states allowed NPs to practice independently, while others mandated some physician involvement (collaborative or supervisory). With PAs, most states required that a physician be physically present (or electronically available) when a PA treated a patient. In addition, many states allowed NPs to prescribe all medications independent of physician supervision, while the ability of PAs to prescribe medications was much more limited. However, the Balanced Budget Act of 1997 removed many of the limitations imposed by individual states. Today, both NPs and PAs are allowed to practice without the immediate availability of a supervising physician. Note, however, that NPs are allowed to practice under their own licenses, while PAs must practice under the license of a physician.

The reimbursement of APPs, like all reimbursement for healthcare services, is complicated by the fact that many different third-party payers use different payment methodologies. For the purposes of this case, assume that all payers use the same system as Medicare, which recognizes several different situations in which APPs deliver services.

In general, Medicare pays APPs in all settings 85 percent of the physician's fee schedule. Thus, if an NP provided a service that would result in a $100 payment to a physician, the NP would be paid $85. However, there are two important exceptions to this rule. First, if the APP and physician both see the patient during an office visit, the combined work of both the APP and physician is reimbursed at 100 percent of the physician fee schedule. But if the patient service is a procedure (as opposed to a visit) and the work is done primarily by the APP, the 85 percent rule applies. Second, APPs are paid at a 100 percent rate if the service provided is "incident to" a previous visit or service provided by a physician. This provision requires that the physician be physically on-site and that the service provided by the APP be related to a diagnosis made earlier by a physician. Note that incident-to billing only applies to services provided in offices and clinics as opposed to services provided in hospitals. In effect, these rules mean that most APP billings in offices and clinics are at the 100 percent rate, so average APP reimbursement falls closer to 100 percent than to 85 percent of the physician rate.

The effect of APPs on physician costs and revenues is highly variable. After some acclimation time, which is required for the APP to become fully productive, several financial effects are realized. First, the physician becomes more productive (sees more patients) because the APPs can provide the service for a portion of the visit that is billed by the physician. On average nationwide, this increase in the number of billed visits by the physician is estimated to be 10 to 15 percent. Second, the physician's average reimbursement amount increases because the APP is handling the less complex cases. The national average impact on physician billing amount is estimated to be 5 to 10 percent. Finally, the APP can see patients independently and bill for those services. On average, APPs see 10 to 20 percent fewer patients than do physicians. In addition, because some of these visits are joint with the physician and billed by the physician, the APP can bill only for the remaining visits, which represent 85 to 90 percent of the total visits. Of course, the extent to which these effects are realized depends on demand (volume). The greater the demand for physician services, the faster an APP can become fully productive and the greater the impact on physician productivity and reimbursement amounts.

At this time, the Practice does not use APPs. However, Dr. Kim believes that APPs can play an important role in many, if not all, of the Practice's clinics. As a start, three clinics have been identified for evaluation: the outpatient surgery preoperative and postoperative clinic, the internal medicine (family practice) clinic, and the eldercare clinic. Dr. Kim then developed the selected data regarding each clinic's physician staffing, productivity, revenues, and costs (shown in exhibit 5.1). For example, the preoperative and postoperative clinic has 2.5 physician FTEs (full-time equivalents) who handle 7,560 patient visits annually, which generate $894,580 of revenue (collections). Annual compensation for the physician FTEs totals $510,000.

You have been hired as a consultant by the Practice to look into the use of APPs. Specifically, Dr. Kim has asked you (1) to estimate the financial impact of using one APP at each of the three clinics and (2) to recommend the type of APP that is most appropriate for each setting. **These tasks are not trivial and might require assumptions and information to supplement the data presented in the case.**

As a start, you conclude that the national financial impact data presented earlier must be modified to reflect the actual impact on physician productivity in the three settings. Next, you plan to estimate how many additional visits might be generated at each clinic if one APP is employed. Then, the impact on costs and revenues must be examined. Of course, it might be possible to use an APP to reduce the number of physician FTEs rather than to increase volume. This outcome should be explored if appropriate. Regarding APPs' costs, annual compensation for both NPs and PAs falls into the $80,000 to $150,000 range, depending on geographic location, clinical setting, and work experience.

One of the keys to the analysis is an estimate of the volumes that could be realized at each clinic should an APP be added. Unfortunately, Dr. Kim has only anecdotal evidence (office watercooler speculation) on future demand. The best estimate is that patient volume at the preoperative and postoperative clinic is increasing at a 15 percent annual rate as outpatient surgery volume increases. The situation at the internal medicine clinic is quite different. There is a several-month backlog in scheduling, and hence an APP could be fully used in a relatively short time. Finally, volume at the eldercare clinic has been sporadic and growing very slowly, so there is some doubt about whether another clinician is needed at this time.

Dr. Kim recognizes that you are working with a minimal amount of hard data. Thus, you must very clearly express and support the assumptions used in your analysis.

EXHIBIT 5.1
Shasta Faculty Practice: Selected Data for Three Outpatient Clinics

Outpatient Surgery Pre- and Post-Op Clinic	
Physician FTEs	2.5
Physician costs	$510,000
Physician fees (collections)	$894,580
Daily patient utilization	36
Number of days per week	5
Number of weeks per year	42
Annual patient utilization	7,560
Number of visits per physician	3,024
Internal Medicine (Family Practice) Clinic	
Physician FTEs	2.0
Physician costs	$293,500
Physician fees (collections)	$533,290
Daily patient utilization	30
Number of days per week	4
Number of weeks per year	46
Annual patient utilization	5,520
Number of visits per physician	2,760
Eldercare Clinic	
Physician FTEs	2.25
Physician costs	$335,000
Physician fees (collections)	$454,219
Daily patient utilization	23
Number of days per week	4
Number of weeks per year	48
Annual patient utilization	4,416
Number of visits per physician	1,963

FTE: full-time equivalent

Note: Most physicians in the Practice receive compensation from the university in addition to the amounts listed in this exhibit.

PART III

COST ALLOCATION

CASE 6

BIG BEND MEDICAL CENTER

COST ALLOCATION CONCEPTS

Big Bend Medical Center is a full-service, not-for-profit, acute care hospital with 325 beds located in Big Bend, Texas. The bulk of Big Bend's facilities are devoted to inpatient care and emergency services. However, a 100,000-square-foot section of the Big Bend complex is devoted to outpatient services. Currently, this space has two primary uses: (1) about 80 percent is used by the Outpatient Clinic, which handles all routine outpatient services offered by the hospital, and (2) 20 percent is used by the Dialysis Center.

The Dialysis Center performs hemodialysis and peritoneal dialysis, which are alternative processes that remove wastes and excess water from the blood for patients with end-stage renal (kidney) disease. In hemodialysis, blood is pumped from the patient's arm through a shunt into a dialysis machine, which uses a cleansing solution and an artificial membrane to perform the functions of a healthy kidney. Then, the cleansed blood is pumped back into the patient through a second shunt. In peritoneal dialysis, the cleansing solution is inserted directly into the abdominal cavity through a catheter. The body naturally cleanses the blood through the peritoneum—a thin membrane that lines the abdominal cavity.

Typically, hemodialysis patients require three dialyses per week, with each treatment lasting about four hours. Patients who use peritoneal dialysis change their own cleansing solutions at home, usually about six times per day. This procedure can be done manually when the patient is active or automatically by machine when the patient is sleeping. However, the patient's overall condition, as well as the positioning of the catheter, must be monitored regularly by nurses and technicians at the Dialysis Center.

Big Bend's cost accounting system allocates facilities overhead costs (which essentially consist of building depreciation and interest on long-term debt) on the basis of square footage. Currently, the facilities cost allocation rate is $15 per square foot, so the facilities cost allocation is 20,000 × $15 = $300,000 for the Dialysis Center and 80,000 × $15 = $1,200,000 for the Outpatient Clinic. All other overhead costs—such as administration, finance, maintenance, and housekeeping—are lumped together and called "general overhead." These costs are allocated at a rate of 10 percent of the revenues of each patient service department, or $0.10 per revenue dollar. The current allocation of general overhead is $270,000 for the Dialysis Center and $1,600,000 for the Outpatient Clinic, which results in total overhead allocations of $570,000 for the Dialysis Center and $2,800,000 for the Outpatient Clinic.

Recent growth in volume of the Outpatient Clinic has created a need for 25 percent more space than is currently assigned. Because the Outpatient Clinic is much larger than the Dialysis Center and its patients need frequent access to other departments within Big Bend, the decision was made to keep the Outpatient Clinic in its current location and move the Dialysis Center to another location to free up space within the Big Bend complex. Such a move would increase the Outpatient Clinic space by 25 percent—to 100,000 square feet.

After attempting to find space for the Dialysis Center within the complex, Big Bend's leadership soon determined that a new 20,000-square-foot building had to be built. This building would be situated three blocks away from the complex, in a location that would be much more convenient for the Dialysis Center patients and employees because of ease of parking. Because the new 20,000 square feet of space can be more efficiently used than the old space, it will allow for some increase in patient volume, although it is unclear whether the move will generate additional dialysis patients.

Construction cost of the new building is estimated at $120 per square foot, for a cost of $2,400,000. In addition, the purchase of land, furniture, and other fittings, along with the relocation of equipment, files, and other items, would cost $1,600,000, for a total cost of $4,000,000 for the new facility. The $4,000,000 cost would be financed by a 7.75 percent, 20-year, first-mortgage loan. When both the principal amount (which can be considered depreciation) and interest are amortized over 20 years, the result is an annual cost of financing of $400,000. Thus, it is possible to estimate the actual annual facilities costs for the new Dialysis Center, something that is not possible for units located within the Big Bend complex.

Exhibit 6.1 contains the projected profit and loss (P&L) statement for the Dialysis Center before adjusting for the move. Big Bend's department heads receive annual bonuses on the basis of each department's contribution to the hospital's bottom line (profit). In the past, only direct costs were considered, but Big Bend's CEO has decided that bonuses will now be based on full (total) costs.

The new approach to awarding bonuses, coupled with the potential increases in indirect cost allocation, is of great concern to John Van Pelt, the director of the Dialysis Center. Under the current allocation of indirect costs (see exhibit 6.1), John would have a reasonable chance of earning an end-of-year bonus, as the forecast puts the Dialysis Center in the black. However, any increase in the indirect cost allocation would likely put him out of the money.

At the next department heads' meeting, John voiced his concern about the impact of any allocation changes on the Dialysis Center's reported profitability. Big Bend's CEO asked the chief financial officer (CFO), Taya Simmons, to conduct an analysis. The CEO said the final allocation was up to Taya, but any allocation changes related to facilities overhead must be made within outpatient services. In other words, any change in facilities cost allocation to the Dialysis Center must be offset by an equal but opposite change in the allocation to the Outpatient Clinic.

To get started, Taya created exhibit 6.2. In creating the exhibit, she assumed that the new Dialysis Center would have the same number of stations as the old one, would serve the same number of patients, and would receive the same reimbursement rates. Direct operating expenses would differ only slightly from the current expenses because the same personnel and equipment would be used. Thus, for all practical purposes, the revenues and direct costs of the Dialysis Center would be unaffected by the move.

The data in exhibit 6.2 for the expanded Outpatient Clinic are based on the assumption that the expansion would allow volume to increase by 25 percent and that both revenues and direct costs would increase by a like amount. Furthermore, to keep the analysis manageable, the overall hospital allocation rates for both facilities costs ($15 per square foot) and general overhead (10 percent of revenues) were assumed to not materially change as a result of the expansion.

In the past, facilities costs were aggregated, so all departments were charged a cost based on the average embedded (historical) cost, regardless of the actual age (or value) of the space occupied. Thus, a basement room with no windows was allocated the same facilities costs (per square foot) as was the fifth-floor executive suite. Because many department heads considered this approach unfair, Taya wanted to explore allocating facilities overhead on a true cost basis. Thus, in her initial allocation, Taya used actual facilities costs as the basis for the allocation to the Dialysis Center. She knew that this initial allocation, which is shown in the Initial Allocation columns in exhibit 6.2, would create some controversy.

John's response to the initial allocation was less than enthusiastic. Specifically, he was concerned about several issues. First and foremost, is it fair to charge the Dialysis Center actual facilities costs for the new location? After all, the move was forced by the Outpatient Clinic, which is being charged for facilities at the lower average allocation rate of $15 per square foot instead of the $20 per square foot applied to the Dialysis Center ($400,000 in annual facilities overhead costs ÷ 20,000 square feet = $20 per square foot). If Big Bend adopted a practice of charging for actual facilities costs while also including indirect costs when calculating bonuses, department heads might be incentivized to resist proposed moves to new (and potentially more efficient) facilities because such moves would result in increased facilities allocations and therefore lower department profitability.

Second, even if the actual cost concept were applied to the Dialysis Center, is the $400,000 annual allocation amount correct? After all, the building has a useful life that is probably significantly longer than 20 years—the life of the loan used to determine the allocation amount. If the true cost concept is applied, what would be the allocation in the twenty-first year, after the mortgage has been paid off?

Finally, although unrelated to facilities overhead, John pointed out that the "revenue" the Dialysis Center "receives" from patients' use of the pharmacy appears to be passed on directly to the pharmacy. That is, the Dialysis Center books $800,000 in annual revenue but is charged a transfer price of $800,000 by the pharmacy for the drugs used. Should this revenue be counted when general overhead allocations are made? To make his point, John discovered that the pharmacy supplies used for dialysis actually cost the pharmacy $400,000, so the pharmacy makes a profit of $400,000 on drugs that are actually "sold" by the Dialysis Center. Before Taya could respond to John's concerns, however, she left Big Bend to be the CFO of a competing investor-owned hospital.

The task of completing the allocation study has been given to you, Big Bend's current administrative fellow. You remember that to be most beneficial, cost allocations should (1) be perceived as fair by the parties involved, (2) allocate overhead costs in a way that reflects each department's use of overhead services, and (3) promote overall cost savings within the organization. However, you also realize that, in practice, cost allocation is very complex and somewhat arbitrary. Some department heads argue that the best approach to overhead allocations is the Marxist approach, which bases allocations on each patient service department's ability to cover overhead costs.

Considering all the relevant issues, you must (1) determine how best to handle the pharmacy revenues and expenses and (2) develop and justify a new indirect cost allocation scheme for outpatient services. Recall that any changes in the total facilities cost allocation must be net neutral to the organization. In other words, changes to the allocation of facilities costs to the Dialysis Center must be offset by an equal but opposite change in the allocation of facilities costs to the Outpatient Clinic.

The allocation of general overhead does not need to be net neutral, and any of the following changes to the accounting for pharmacy revenue and expenses are open for negotiation: (1) exclusion of the pass-through revenue from the sale of pharmaceutical supplies in the allocation of general overhead to the Dialysis Center, (2) a change in the way pharmacy revenues and expenses are recorded (e.g., recording revenue and costs related to pharmacy sales directly by the pharmacy rather than passing through the Dialysis Center), or (3) a change in the transfer price for drugs charged by the pharmacy. Summarize your proposal, including any changes to pharmacy revenues and costs (and therefore, changes in total revenues and expenses for the Dialysis Center), and the final facilities and general overhead allocation amounts in the Alternative Allocation columns in exhibit 6.2. In the Summary section at the bottom of exhibit 6.2, calculate the implied facilities and general overhead allocation rates resulting from your proposed allocation scheme. Be prepared to justify your recommendations at the next department heads' meeting.

EXHIBIT 6.1
Big Bend Medical Center Dialysis Center: Pro Forma P&L Statement Assuming Status Quo

Revenues	
Hemodialysis program	$1,300,000
Peritoneal dialysis program	600,000
Pharmaceutical supplies	800,000
Total revenues	$2,700,000
Direct Expenses	
Salaries and benefits	$ 900,000
Pharmaceutical supplies	800,000
Other medical/administrative supplies	100,000
Utilities	80,000
Equipment lease expense	120,000
Other expenses	100,000
Total expenses	$2,100,000
Net gain (loss) before indirect costs	$ 600,000
Indirect Expenses	
Facilities costs	$ 300,000
General overhead	270,000
Total overhead costs	$ 570,000
Net profit	$ 30,000

Note: Pharmacy revenues are based on reimbursement amounts, not costs.

EXHIBIT 6.2
Big Bend Medical Center: Dialysis Center (DC) and Outpatient Clinic (OC) Summary Projections

P&L Statements:			With Expansion			
	Without Expansion		*Initial Allocation*		*Alternative Allocation*	
	DC	*OC*	*DC*	*OC*	*DC*	*OC*
Revenues/Direct Costs						
Total revenues	$ 2,700,000	$16,000,000	$ 2,700,000	$20,000,000	$	$20,000,000
Direct expenses	2,100,000	9,833,155	2,100,000	12,291,444		12,291,444
Contribution margin	$ 600,000	$ 6,166,845	$ 600,000	$ 7,708,556	$	$ 7,708,556
Contribution margin as a % of revenues	22.2%	38.5%	22.2%	38.5%	%	38.5%
Indirect Costs						
Facilities costs	$ 300,000	$ 1,200,000	$ 400,000	$ 1,500,000	$	$
General overhead	270,000	1,600,000	270,000	2,000,000		2,000,000
Total overhead	$ 570,000	$ 2,800,000	$ 670,000	$ 3,500,000	$	$
Net profit (loss)	$ 30,000	$ 3,366,845	($ 70,000)	$ 4,208,556	$	$
Net profit as a % of revenues	1.1%	21.0%	(2.6%)	21.0%	%	%
Summary of Overhead Allocation and Implied Allocation Rates:						
Facilities Cost Allocation:	$ 300,000	$ 1,200,000	$ 400,000	$ 1,500,000	$	$
Square footage	20,000	80,000	20,000	100,000	20,000	100,000
Implied facilities costs per square foot (facilities cost allocation ÷ square footage)	$ 15	$ 15	$ 20	$ 15	$	$
General Overhead Allocation:	$ 270,000	$ 1,600,000	$ 270,000	$ 2,000,000		$ 2,000,000
Implied general overhead costs as a % of revenue (general overhead allocation ÷ total revenues × 100)	10.0%	10.0%	10.0%	10.0%	%	10.0%

Note: The term *contribution margin* as used here means the amount available to cover overhead costs, as opposed to the traditional meaning of the amount available to cover fixed costs.

CASE 7

EAGAN FAMILY PRACTICE

COST ALLOCATION METHODS

EAGAN FAMILY PRACTICE is a medical practice with four locations in the Minneapolis–St. Paul area. The clinical staff consists of 20 physicians—all of whom practice in one or more areas of family medicine—and 46 advanced practice providers and nurses. Eagan is organized into three patient service departments: Adult Medicine, Obstetrics, and Pediatrics. Supporting these patient service departments are the Administration, Facilities, and Finance departments. Exhibit 7.1 shows Eagan's summary revenue and cost projections by department for the coming year.

As part of a much-needed overhaul of the cost allocation process, Eagan contracted with a major accounting firm to estimate the amount of services provided by the support departments to each other and to each patient service department. The intent of the study was to provide data that would help Eagan develop a better cost allocation system to replace the outdated, arbitrary system currently in use. The results of this study are shown in exhibit 7.2. Although expressed as percentages of the total dollar amount of support provided to other departments (instead of the more typical cost allocation rates), the data in exhibit 7.2 are based on an extensive study using sound managerial accounting techniques. Thus, both senior management and department heads at Eagan are comfortable with the resulting allocation percentages. **(Hint: To ensure that you apply the percentages properly in your analysis, pay attention to note 2 at the bottom of exhibit 7.2.)**

The second step in the cost allocation process-improvement initiative is to choose the allocation method. Four allocation methods are under consideration: direct, step-down, double apportionment, and reciprocal. Jerry Silverman, Eagan's chief financial officer, has asked Ashley Matson, the administrative resident at Eagan, to conduct a study and make a recommendation on the best allocation method. This task can be approached in several ways, but Ashley has decided to examine by doing. She plans to use the data in exhibits 7.1 and 7.2 to determine the overhead cost allocations under each allocation method. Afterward, she can compare and contrast the results.

Of course, the final decision cannot be made without considering the costs involved in implementing each allocation method. When Ashley asked Jerry about the costs inherent in each allocation method, Jerry said, "I don't know! Assume that the direct method is the least costly, the reciprocal method is the most costly, and the other two fall somewhere in between." He also expects Ashley to make some judgments on the relative profitability of the patient service departments under the recommended allocation system.

Ashley began her analysis by reviewing the allocation methods presented in her old healthcare finance textbook. She had no problem remembering basic cost allocation concepts, but she did hit two snags. The first problem was that the textbook did not describe the double apportionment method. However, after a little research, Ashley discovered that the double apportionment method is a slightly more complicated version of the step-down method. In the first apportionment, support provided by each service department to the other service departments as well as to the patient service departments is recognized. Because some costs remain in the support departments after the first apportionment, a second apportionment, which applies the step-down method, moves all remaining support department costs to the patient service departments. Thus, in the double apportionment method, service department support to all other service departments is recognized, whereas in the pure step-down method, service department support is recognized only to "downstream" service departments.

Here's how Ashley assumed that the double apportionment method would be applied to Eagan. (There are alternative ways in which this allocation method can be applied.) First, direct Administration costs would be allocated to the other five departments (two support and three patient service). Second, direct Facilities costs would be allocated to all other departments (including Administration and Finance). Third, direct Finance costs would be allocated to all other departments (including Administration and Facilities). After these three allocations are completed, the first apportionment is finished. Some costs remain in the support departments—the allocations to the other support departments from the first apportionment—so a second apportionment is necessary. The second apportionment is conducted using the step-down method as it is normally applied, except that the application of the first apportionment means that the starting cost pool values are much lower.

The second problem Ashley faced was that she did not know how to perform the reciprocal allocation. One method is to use simultaneous equations—but higher mathematics has never been Ashley's strong suit—and another method uses an iterative approach. Fortunately, Ashley had recently read an article in *Accounting Monthly* discussing an Excel model that uses the iterative approach to perform reciprocal allocation. To help with the analysis, Ashley modified the magazine's model by using Eagan's numbers to calculate the allocation not only for the reciprocal method but also for the other three methods.

Put yourself in Ashley's shoes. Complete her assigned task and prepare a report to present to Eagan's executive committee. In addition, assess the sensitivity of the results to (1) the relative sizes of the direct costs at each support department and (2) the amount of support provided by the support departments to each other. Exhibit 7.3 contains the values you may use in your sensitivity analysis.

EXHIBIT 7.1
Eagan Family Practice: Departmental Revenue and Cost Projections

Revenues	
Adult Medicine	$14,000,000
Obstetrics	8,000,000
Pediatrics	4,000,000
Total revenues	$26,000,000
Direct Costs	
Patient Services	
Adult Medicine	$ 7,000,000
Obstetrics	5,100,000
Pediatrics	2,200,000
Subtotal	$14,300,000
Support	
Administration	$ 2,000,000
Facilities	5,400,000
Finance	2,500,000
Subtotal	$ 9,900,000
Total expenses	$24,200,000
Pretax profit	$ 1,800,000

EXHIBIT 7.2
Eagan Family Practice: Allocation Percentages

	Percentage of Services Provided by		
Services Provided to	*Administration*	*Facilities*	*Finance*
Administration	—	5%	5%
Facilities	10%	—	5
Finance	10	10	—
Adult Medicine	35	55	50
Obstetrics	20	10	25
Pediatrics	25	20	15
Total	100%	100%	100%
Percentage to support departments	20%	15%	10%
Percentage to patient service departments	80%	85%	90%

Notes: 1. The allocation percentages are based on a two-year analysis of the actual services provided by the support departments to other departments.

2. To use the percentages to perform an allocation, you may have to adjust them to ensure that the entire amount of the cost pool is allocated. To illustrate, in the direct method, all of Administration's costs ($500,000) have to be allocated directly in a single allocation to the three patient service departments. If the raw percentages were used, only 35% + 20% + 25% = 80% of the cost pool would be allocated, so the allocation percentages have to be adjusted so that 80 percent represents the entire allocation (100 percent). Thus, instead of a 35 percent allocation to Adult Medicine, its adjusted allocation is 35%/80% = 43.75%. In a similar manner, the adjusted allocation to Obstetrics is 20%/80% = 25%, while the adjusted allocation to Pediatrics is 25%/80% = 31.25%. When done correctly, the adjusted percentages must sum to 100%: 43.75% + 25% + 31.25% = 100%.

EXHIBIT 7.3
Eagan Family Practice: Sensitivity Analysis Values

Sensitivity to Changes in Relative Overhead Costs:

New Direct Expenses for Calculation 1	
Administration	$5,400,000
Facilities	2,000,000
Finance	2,500,000
Total overhead expenses	$9,900,000
New Direct Expenses for Calculation 2	
Administration	$2,000,000
Facilities	2,500,000
Finance	5,400,000
Total overhead expenses	$9,900,000

Sensitivity to Allocation Percentages:

	Percentage of Services Provided by		
Services Provided to	*Administration*	*Facilities*	*Finance*
Administration	—	25%	20%
Facilities	30%	—	20
Finance	30	25	—
Adult Medicine	18	32	33
Obstetrics	10	6	17
Pediatrics	12	12	10
Total	100%	100%	100%
Percentage to support departments	60%	50%	40%
Percentage to patient service departments	40%	50%	60%

CASE

8

DALLAS HEALTH NETWORK

ACTIVITY-BASED COSTING ANALYSIS

DALLAS HEALTH NETWORK (the Network), which consists of five medical group practices, is a subsidiary of not-for-profit Dallas Health System (the System). The Network includes both primary care and specialty physicians, with an emphasis on obstetrics/gynecology, eldercare, and pediatrics. Prior to the founding of the Network, the five practices operated independently.

The Network has three practice locations, each staffed with a mix of primary care and specialist physicians. Although the Network itself is only marginally profitable, it is an important contributor to the profitability of the System because it generates a large amount of revenues from referrals for both inpatient admissions and inpatient and outpatient ancillary services. In fact, each $1 of revenue generated within the Network is estimated to lead to $8 of inpatient and ancillary revenues to the System. By limiting the amount of ancillary services provided at the three Network locations, patients are forced (or at least encouraged) to use other System facilities for such services.

Still, some ancillary services are best performed at the Network locations for one or more of the following reasons: lower costs, increased physician efficiency, and improved patient convenience and hence better CAHPS (Consumer Assessment of Healthcare Providers and Systems) scores. For example, one of the practice locations now has a diagnostic imaging capability. When the scanner was moved from another facility to the Network location, volume increased, costs decreased, and both physician and patient satisfaction improved. (For more information on the CAHPS program, see www.ahrq.gov/cahps/about-cahps/index.html.)

The proposal currently being considered by the Network is to provide ultrasound services at the Network locations. Preliminary analysis indicates that two approaches are most suitable. Alternative 1 involves the purchase of one ultrasound machine for each of the Network's three locations. Patients would schedule appointments, generally at the clinic they are using, for preset times on specified days of the week. Then, a full-time ultrasound technician would travel from one location to another to administer the tests as scheduled. Alternative 2, on the other hand, involves the purchase of only one ultrasound machine, but patient scheduling would be the same. The machine would be mounted in a van that the technician would drive to each of the three Network locations. Most of the operating costs of the two alternatives are identical, but Alternative 2 has the added cost of operating the van and setting up the machine after each move.

The two alternatives differ substantially in capital investment costs because Alternative 1 requires three ultrasound machines, at a cost of $100,000 each, whereas Alternative 2 requires only one machine. However, Alternative 2 requires a van, which, with necessary modifications, would cost $40,000. Thus, the capital costs for Alternative 1 total 3 × $100,000 = $300,000, whereas the costs for Alternative 2 amount to only $100,000 + $40,000 = $140,000.

Because the two alternatives have different operating costs, a proper cost analysis of the two alternatives must include both capital investment and operating costs. The Network financial staff, which in reality is the System financial staff, considered several methods for estimating the operating costs of each alternative. After much discussion, the chief financial officer (CFO) decided that the activity-based costing (ABC) method would be best. Furthermore, an ad hoc task force was assigned to perform the cost analysis.

To begin the ABC analysis, the task force had to develop the activities involved in the two alternatives. This task was accomplished by conducting walk-throughs of the entire process from the standpoint of the patient, the ultrasound technician, and the billing and collections department. The results are shown in exhibit 8.1. A review of the activities confirms that all except one—consisting of transportation, setup, and breakdown—are applicable to both alternatives.

The next step in the ABC process is to detail the costs associated with each activity. This step uses financial, operational, and volume data, along with the appropriate cost driver for each activity, to estimate resource consumption. Note that traditional costing, which often focuses on department-level costs, typically first deals with direct costs and then allocates indirect (overhead) costs proportionally according to a predetermined allocation rate. In ABC costing, the activities required to produce some service, including both direct and indirect, are estimated simultaneously. For example, exhibit 8.1 contains activities that entail direct costs (such as technician time) and activities that entail indirect costs (such as billing and collection). Although the ABC method is more complex and hence costlier than the traditional method, it is the only way to estimate, more or less accurately, the costs of individual services.

Activity cost detail on a per-procedure basis is contained in exhibit 8.2. Each activity is assigned a cost driver that is most highly correlated with the actual utilization of resources. Then, the number of driver units, along with the cost per unit, is estimated for each activity. The product of the number of units and the cost per unit gives the cost of each activity. Finally, the activity costs are summed to obtain the total per-procedure cost.

Many of the activity costs cannot be calculated without an estimate of the number of ultrasounds that will be performed. The best estimate is that 50 procedures would be done each week, regardless of which alternative is chosen. Assuming the technician works 48 weeks per year, the annual volume estimate is 2,400 procedures. Of course, one factor that complicates the analysis is that a much greater total volume can be accommodated under Alternative 1 (with three machines) than with Alternative 2 (with only one machine). However, to keep the initial analysis manageable, the decision was made to assume the same annual volume regardless of the alternative chosen.

Other costs are thought to be relevant to the decision. First, in addition to the purchasing and operating (primarily consisting of fuel expenses) costs of the van, the estimated annual vehicle maintenance costs are $1,000. Furthermore, annual maintenance costs on each of the three ultrasound machines under Alternative 1 are estimated at $1,000, whereas the annual maintenance costs for the single machine under Alternative 2 are estimated higher, at $1,500, because of added wear and tear. The manufacturer of the ultrasound machines has indicated that a discount may be available if three machines, as opposed to only one, are purchased. The amount of the discount is somewhat uncertain, although 5 percent has been mentioned.

Finally, to get a rough estimate of the total annual costs over the life of the equipment, assumptions about the useful life of the ultrasound machines and the van have to be made. Although somewhat controversial, the decision was made to assume a five-year life for both the ultrasound machines and the van and that the value of these assets would be negligible at the end of five years.

You are the chair of the Network's ad hoc task force. Your charge is to evaluate the two alternatives and to make a recommendation on which one to accept, assuming that revenues would be identical for the two alternatives, and hence the decision can be made solely on the basis of costs. As part of the analysis, the costs of the two alternatives must be estimated on a per-procedure basis and an annual basis. In addition, any relevant qualitative factors must be considered before the recommendation is made.

To keep the base case analysis manageable, the task force was instructed to assume that the operating costs remain constant over the useful life of the equipment. For comparative purposes, this assumption is not too egregious because the activities are roughly the same for both alternatives and, hence, inflation would have a somewhat neutral impact on the cost comparison.

In addition, the System's CFO has asked the task force to perform some sensitivity (scenario) analyses. He is concerned about the accuracy of the cost detail inputs. Although he is confident about many of the estimates, he thinks others are arbitrary. Those activity cost inputs considered to be most uncertain are supplies cost per unit; billing and collection cost per unit; general administration cost per unit; and transportation, setup, and breakdown cost per unit.

Thus, first, the task force has to redo the analysis assuming that these inputs are higher than the base case values by 10 and 20 percent. Activity cost inputs less than the base case values could also be examined, but the critical issue here is not to underestimate the total costs involved in the two alternatives. Second, the task force has to determine what would happen to the cost estimates if the useful life of the capital equipment were as short as three years or as long as seven years. Another concern was that the useful life of the equipment depended on the alternative chosen; that is, there would be less wear and tear under Alternative 1 than under Alternative 2. Finally, the task force has to assess the impact of a purchase discount—would the discount amount influence the ultimate decision?

You believe that performing a sensitivity analysis on the number of procedures would be helpful, but you realize this task would require recalculation of the per-unit cost inputs, an effort thought to be too time-consuming to undertake at this point in the analysis.

EXHIBIT 8.1
Dallas Health Network: Activities Associated with Alternatives 1 and 2

1. Appointment scheduling
2. Patient check-in
3. Ultrasound testing
4. Patient check-out
5. Film processing
6. Film reading
7. Billing and collection
8. General administration
9. Transportation, setup, and breakdown (Alternative 2 only)

EXHIBIT 8.2
Dallas Health Network: Activity Cost Detail

Activity	*Cost Driver*	*Volume*	*Cost per Unit*
Appointment scheduling	Receptionist time	3 minutes	$ 0.20
Patient check-in	Receptionist time	5 minutes	0.20
Ultrasound testing	Technician time	30 minutes	0.40
	Physician time	1.5 minutes	3.00
	Supplies	per procedure	9.00
Patient check-out	Receptionist time	5 minutes	0.20
Film processing	Technician time	10 minutes	0.40
Film reading	Contract terms	per procedure	40.00
Billing and collection	Overhead costs	per procedure	6.80
General administration	Overhead costs	per procedure	1.25
Transportation, setup, and breakdown	Technician time	18 minutes	0.50

Notes:
1. Physician time for testing (15 minutes) is needed for one of every 10 patients.
2. Supplies consist of linen, probe cover, gel, film, and print paper.
3. There are no radiologists in the Network. Films will be read by the hospital's radiologists at a contract fee of $40 per procedure.
4. Billing and collection costs are based on an average cost per medical services bill.
5. General administration costs are based on an estimate of facilities and other administrative costs.
6. Transportation, setup, and breakdown are based on 10 procedures per day and include vehicle operating costs, excluding maintenance.

PART IV
PRICING, PLANNING, AND BUDGETING

CASE 9

CAMBRIDGE TRANSPLANT CENTER

MARGINAL COST PRICING ANALYSIS

CAMBRIDGE TRANSPLANT CENTER (the Center), which is part of University Healthcare System, is a regional leader in the very intense and medically sophisticated area of organ transplantation. All transplants are performed at Cambridge General Hospital, the 400-bed flagship of University.

The administrative director of the Center, Josh Zimmerman, has been on the job for 10 years, during which time significant growth has occurred in both the number of transplant programs and the volume of procedures performed. When Josh joined the Center, he was put in charge of a kidney transplant program that averaged 60 transplants per year and a heart transplant program that performed 40 transplants annually. Today, the Center performs more than 500 transplants per year, including transplants from liver, lung, and pancreas programs.

Of all the Center's organ programs, the liver transplant program is the most successful in terms of volume and revenue. Last year, volume totaled 120 transplants, bringing in more than $50 million in total revenues. This year, Josh is optimistic that the liver program can do even better. However, he knows that increased volume is largely dependent on the number of organ donors and on his success in negotiating a new contract with Lifecare Transplant Network (LTNET), the largest transplant benefits company in the nation.

Although most health insurers can identify those patients who are good candidates for transplant services, only the largest health insurers have the expertise to manage the transplant process. Transplants are relatively rare compared with other, more conventional medical procedures. However, the costs to insurers for transplant services are typically very large—usually in the six- to seven-figure range. To ensure the best and most cost-effective management of transplant services, most insurers outsource transplant management to companies that specialize in these services, such as LTNET.

Contracting for transplant services is uniquely complex because of the sophistication of the medical procedures involved. Transplant services consist of five phases: (1) patient evaluation, (2) patient care while awaiting surgery, (3) organ procurement, (4) surgery and the attendant inpatient stay, and (5) one year of follow-up visits. The costs involved in Phase 1 are relatively simple to estimate, but the resource utilization, and hence costs, of the remaining phases can be extremely variable because they differ based on patient acuity and surgical outcomes.

Historically, reimbursement for transplant services has been handled in a number of ways. Initially, many transplant providers bundled all five phases and offered insurers a single, global rate. This method simplified the contracting process, but the rate set for this method was often chosen on the basis of building market share rather than on covering costs. Indeed, many institutions could not even estimate with any confidence the true costs of providing transplant services.

Ironically, success in gaining market share usually increases the financial risk of the transplant program because higher volumes increase the likelihood of attracting higher-acuity patients. Furthermore, changes in the organ allocation system have promoted the acceptance of sicker patients into transplant programs. Although the total costs associated with all phases of a liver transplant average about $500,000, the amount can more than quadruple if the patient requires a re-transplant or if other complications occur. Because of this extreme variability in costs, outlier protection is a critical aspect of contract negotiations if the reimbursement methodology is a fixed prospective rate, such as a global rate.

The LTNET contract requires the approval of Dr. Anjali Desai, the newly appointed surgical director of the liver transplant program. Fortunately, like Josh, Dr. Desai is enthusiastic about turning the liver transplant program into one of the largest in the country and is motivated to secure the contract. In his second meeting with Dr. Desai, Josh discussed the specifics of the current contract negotiations. Phases 1, 2, and 5 will be reimbursed at a set discount from charges. Furthermore, to reduce the amount of financial risk borne by the Center, Phase 3 (organ procurement) will be reimbursed on a cost basis, which makes sense because the cost of Phase 3 is almost completely uncontrollable by the Center. Thus, the primary focus of the negotiations, and the make-or-break part of the contract, is the reimbursement amount for Phase 4. (For more information on organ procurement, see the United Network for Organ Sharing website at www.unos.org.)

Phase 4 costs are divided into two categories: hospital costs and physician costs. Physician reimbursement has already been agreed on, with LTNET committing to pay a fixed amount per physician work relative value unit (RVU). Thus, the primary matter at hand involves only Phase 4 hospital costs. To aid in the negotiations, Josh compiled the Phase 4 hospital costs of the 12 most recent liver transplant patients. These data are presented in exhibit 9.1.

Dr. Desai was amazed when she read the numbers. A total average cost of $119,805 for 19 days average length of stay (ALOS) translates to a per diem average cost of more than $6,000. She was sure that LTNET would not be willing to sign a contract that paid the hospital $120,000 (or more) to cover Phase 4 hospital costs. Thus, she suggested that Josh reexamine the cost structure to see if these costs could be reduced.

At first glance, it appeared that a large cost savings could be realized by merely reducing ALOS. For example, Phase 4 hospital costs associated with a particular patient could be reduced by more than $12,000 by decreasing ALOS by two days. However, further analysis revealed that the costs associated with Phase 4 are not a linear function of ALOS. Internal studies at the Center indicated that the first day of Phase 4 is usually the most costly and the last day is usually the least costly. Indeed, roughly 70 percent of Phase 4 costs occur in the first 24 hours of hospitalization.

When lowering Phase 4 hospital costs appeared to be difficult, Josh decided to pursue a different strategy. He believed that economies of scale are present in liver transplants, and hence the marginal cost of each transplant is lower than the average cost. Thus, he proposed that the Phase 4 hospital reimbursement amount be based on marginal rather than total (full) costs.

You have been hired as a consultant to recommend a fixed reimbursement amount (the base rate) to propose during the contract negotiations for Phase 4 hospital services. To help in the analysis, Josh has indicated that approximately 60 percent of nursing, ancillary, operating room, and laboratory costs are fixed. The remaining costs—radiology, drug, and other services—are predominantly variable. Furthermore, current payers are reimbursing the hospital at roughly $140,000 for Phase 4 services.

The Center has sufficient capacity to handle about 30 more transplants before fixed costs would increase by a meaningful amount. If marginal volume exceeds 30 transplants, the best estimate is that fixed costs would increase somewhere between 15 and 25 percent.

In addition, you have been asked to recommend a method for handling outliers, including the threshold amount and additional reimbursement scheme. Other programs within the Center use two methods for outlier payments. One method is to charge an additional per diem amount based on a length-of-stay threshold. Alternatively, some percentage of costs above the threshold can be charged when a cost threshold is reached. (For more information on how Medicare treats outliers, go to www.cms.hhs.gov/mlngeninfo and search "inpatient outliers.")

As you think about the problem at hand, several other issues will come to mind. First, is it useful to identify the underlying cost structure of the Phase 4 hospital services? (It might help in thinking about the relevant issues.) Second, should the hospital worry about a long-term pricing strategy, or is it sufficient to think only of the first-year contract? Finally, if the price is set significantly lower than the average reimbursement amount paid by current payers, what impact would that have on future negotiations with those payers?

EXHIBIT 9.1
Cambridge Transplant Center: Phase 4 Hospital Costs (in Millions of Dollars)

Patient	*Age (years)*	*LOS (days)*	*Total Costs*	*Nursing Cost*	*Ancillary Cost*	*OR Cost*	*Lab Cost*	*Radiology Cost*	*Drug Cost*	*Other Costs*
A	61	25	$141,092	$10,261	$65,416	$6,770	$13,712	$1,483	$20,992	$22,458
B	56	15	139,306	11,969	63,668	8,501	7,409	2,261	24,504	20,994
C	42	12	74,259	6,939	33,661	3,128	5,279	668	6,964	17,620
D	52	13	115,349	7,221	54,063	5,779	6,112	903	7,638	33,633
E	12	26	172,613	28,205	72,204	6,847	10,550	1,766	23,061	29,980
F	59	22	83,807	16,858	33,474	4,654	6,211	1,397	9,698	11,515
G	41	25	136,060	9,645	63,208	6,489	13,091	1,382	20,127	22,118
H	35	17	139,308	11,969	63,669	8,501	7,409	2,261	24,505	20,994
I	52	12	74,259	6,939	33,660	3,128	5,280	668	6,964	17,620
J	38	13	115,348	7,221	54,063	5,778	6,111	903	7,639	33,633
K	59	25	166,224	26,909	69,657	6,765	10,061	1,677	22,007	29,148
L	60	21	80,034	15,629	32,202	4,531	5,937	1,293	9,122	11,320
Mean	*47*	*19*	*$119,805*	*$13,314*	*$53,245*	*$5,906*	*$8,097*	*$1,389*	*$15,268*	*$22,586*

LOS: length of stay; OR: operating room

CASE 10

CASCADES MENTAL HEALTH CLINIC

VARIANCE ANALYSIS

Cascades Mental Health Clinic is a not-for-profit multidisciplinary mental health provider that offers both inpatient and outpatient services on a full-risk (capitated) basis to members of managed care plans. Its clinical staff consists primarily of psychiatrists, psychologists, psychiatric nurses, social workers, and chemical dependency counselors. Currently, Cascades has major contracts with two large managed care organizations in its service area: Pacific Care Plan and Seattle Health Plan. Each of these organizations has both commercial and Medicare health maintenance organization (HMO) contracts with Cascades. Thus, in total, there are four separate product lines.

Cascades is partially funded by state and local governments. The agreement with the funding agencies is that funds received are to be used to cover overhead and capital expenses. Furthermore, expenses for drugs and other medical and administrative supplies are billed separately to the HMOs at cost. Thus, overhead and supplies expenses are not part of this budget, which means that the analysis focuses on clinical labor expenses. If the assumption is made that other payment mechanisms cover overhead, capital expenses, and supplies at cost, then the profitability of Cascades is solely a function of its ability to create revenues that exceed labor costs. Thus, its operating budget focuses on enrollment, per member premiums, utilization, and labor costs.

Exhibit 10.1 lists the assumptions used to prepare Cascades's 2022 operating budget. Note that the four product lines are expected to provide a total of 4,551,000 member-months of revenue during 2022. Also, note that each product line has a different per member per month (PMPM) payment (premium) amount. Exhibit 10.1 also shows expected admission (for inpatients), referral rate (for outpatients), and labor cost and utilization data for each product line. Because of the unique employment arrangements between Cascades and its clinical staff, in which the staff are paid on the basis of the number of patient service units provided, clinical labor costs are virtually all variable, and hence labor costs are not identified as fixed or variable.

Exhibit 10.2 contains the forecasted 2022 budget. In essence, the data in exhibit 10.1 are used to forecast revenues and costs, both in the aggregate and by product line. Overall, Cascades expected to earn a total profit of $419,379 on the four product lines in 2022.

During the first quarter of 2022, Cascades's managers noted a higher utilization rate than budgeted. To add to their concern, the monthly enrollment figures supplied by the contracting managed care plans were less than those budgeted. Together, these trends indicated lower revenues and higher per-enrollee costs, and hence lower profits, than forecasted in exhibit 10.2. These concerns were borne out when the first-quarter profits came in under budget. To help stem the adverse trend, the managers instituted a utilization management system in which all inpatient stays were required to be approved by the medical director, a senior staff psychiatrist. In addition, Cascades made midyear changes to its commercial premiums that increased the average premiums for the year.

Unfortunately, the action taken was too little, too late to save the year. Exhibit 10.3 provides operating results for 2022, and exhibit 10.4 shows the realized aggregate and product line profit and loss (P&L) statements. A quick review of exhibit 10.4 reveals that the signals conveyed by the first-quarter data were indeed correct; although 2022 ended with a profit, the profit was much less than the amount forecasted.

When the results were submitted to Cascades's CEO, Jennifer Jacobs, she grimaced and said, "I knew it was coming, but I did not expect the profit number to be so low." It was immediately apparent to Jennifer that Cascades could not afford similar results in 2023. She knew that something had to be done, but the best course of action was not clear.

To help plan for next year, Jennifer asked Cascades's finance and accounting department head, Rob Maldonado, to perform a variance analysis on the data to help identify the problems that led to the poor financial results for 2022. Unfortunately, Rob's area of expertise is dealing with lenders and other capital suppliers, so he passed the assignment on to you, a newly hired financial analyst.

To start the analysis, you created a diagram (exhibit 10.5) to help understand variance analysis. (Note that this diagram is generic and has not been customized for this case.) Furthermore, you recognize that because the volume variance consists of differences in both enrollment and utilization, it is necessary to create two flexible budgets: one flexed (adjusted) for actual enrollment only, and the other flexed for both actual enrollment and actual utilization. In addition, to help with the calculations, you jotted down an equation list for calculating variances (exhibit 10.6). (Note that not all of the equations listed are necessarily applicable to this analysis.)

Of course, both Jennifer and Rob are more concerned with what the numbers mean than what the numbers are. Therefore, your variance analysis should include a great deal of interpretation along with the numbers. Finally, because you want to use this assignment to help advance your career at Cascades, you plan to go one step further by offering recommendations for management action along with the numbers and their interpretation.

EXHIBIT 10.1
Cascades Mental Health Clinic: 2022 Operating Budget Assumptions

Expected Enrollment (member-months)

PC Commercial	3,365,000
PC Medicare	469,000
SH Commercial	502,000
SH Medicare	215,000
Total	4,551,000

Expected Premium Data (per member per month)

PC Commercial	$0.70
PC Medicare	0.85
SH Commercial	0.75
SH Medicare	0.80

Expected Labor Data per Admission or Session

	Inpatient		*Outpatient*	
	No. of Hours	*Hourly Rate*	*No. of Hours*	*Hourly Rate*
PC Commercial	53.74	$35	1.04	$100
PC Medicare	68.43	35	1.30	100
SH Commercial	47.77	35	1.15	100
SH Medicare	56.86	35	1.14	100

EXHIBIT 10.1
Cascades Mental Health Clinic: 2022 Operating Budget Assumptions (continued)

Expected Utilization and Total Labor Cost Data

		Inpatient			Outpatient			
Plan Type	*Avg. No. of Members (in Thousands)*	*Admission Rate*	*Cost per Admission*	*Total Costs*	*Referral Rate*	*Cost per Session*	*Total Costs*	*Total*
PC:								
Commercial	280.417	3.81	$1,881	$2,009,639	2.00	$104	$58,327	$2,067,966
Medicare	39.083	3.96	2,395	370,671	2.00	130	10,162	380,833
Total	319.500			$2,380,310			$68,489	$2,448,799
SH:								
Commercial	41.833	3.89	$1,672	$ 272,085	2.00	$115	$ 9,622	$ 281,707
Medicare	17.917	4.17	1,990	148,681	2.00	114	4,085	152,766
Total	59.750			$ 420,766			$13,707	$ 434,473
Grand total	379.250			$2,801,076			$82,196	$2,883,272

PC: Pacific Care; SH: Seattle Health

EXHIBIT 10.2 Cascades Mental Health Clinic: 2022 Operating Budget

Expected Product Line and Aggregate Profits

	PC		SH		
	Commercial	*Medicare*	*Commercial*	*Medicare*	*Total*
Revenue	$2,335,500	$ 398,650	$ 376,500	$172,000	$3,302,650
Costs	2,067,964	380,836	281,709	152,763	2,883,271
Profit	$ 287,536	$ 17,814	$ 94,791	$ 19,237	$ 419,379
Margin	12.3%	4.5%	25.2%	11.2%	12.7%

EXHIBIT 10.3 Cascades Mental Health Clinic: 2022 Operating Results

Actual Enrollment (member-months)

PC Commercial	3,073,133
PC Medicare	485,000
SH Commercial	547,105
SH Medicare	257,000
Total	4,362,238

Actual Premium Data (per member per month)

PC Commercial	$0.75
PC Medicare	0.85
SH Commercial	0.80
SH Medicare	0.80

Actual Labor Data per Admission or Session

	Inpatient		Outpatient	
	No. of Hours	*Hourly Rate*	*No. of Hours*	*Hourly Rate*
PC Commercial	47.32	$38	0.95	$109.50
PC Medicare	58.66	38	1.15	109.50
SH Commercial	52.06	33	0.98	95
SH Medicare	84.85	33	2.00	95

EXHIBIT 10.3
Cascades Mental Health Clinic: 2022 Operating Results (continued)

Actual Utilization and Cost Data

		Inpatient			Outpatient			
Plan Type	*Avg. No. of Members (in Thousands)*	*Admission Rate*	*Cost per Admission*	*Total Costs*	*Referral Rate*	*Cost per Session*	*Total Costs*	*Total*
PC:								
Commercial	256.094	4.33	$1,798	$1,993,782	3.65	$104	$ 97,213	$2,090,996
Medicare	40.417	4.68	2,229	421,615	1.86	126	9,472	431,087
Total	296.511			$2,415,397			$106,685	$2,522,083
SH:								
Commercial	45.592	5.79	$1,718	$ 453,514	3.35	$ 93	$ 14,204	$ 467,719
Medicare	21.417	4.56	2,800	273,448	1.75	190	7,121	280,569
Total	67.009			$ 726,962			$ 21,325	$ 748,288
Grand total	363.520			$3,142,360			$128,011	$3,270,371

Note: These data were generated on a spreadsheet, and hence some rounding differences occur.

EXHIBIT 10.4
Cascades Mental Health Clinic: 2022 Actual P&L Statements

Product Line and Aggregate Profit Results

	PC		*SH*		
	Commercial	*Medicare*	*Commercial*	*Medicare*	*Total*
Revenue	$2,304,850	$ 412,250	$ 437,684	$205,600	$3,360,384
Costs	2,090,996	431,087	467,719	280,569	3,270,371
Profit (loss)	$ 213,584	($ 18,837)	($ 30,035)	($ 74,969)	$ 90,013
Margin	9.3%	(4.6%)	(6.9%)	(36.5%)	2.7%

Note: These data were generated on a spreadsheet, and hence some rounding differences occur.

EXHIBIT 10.5
Variance Analysis Summary

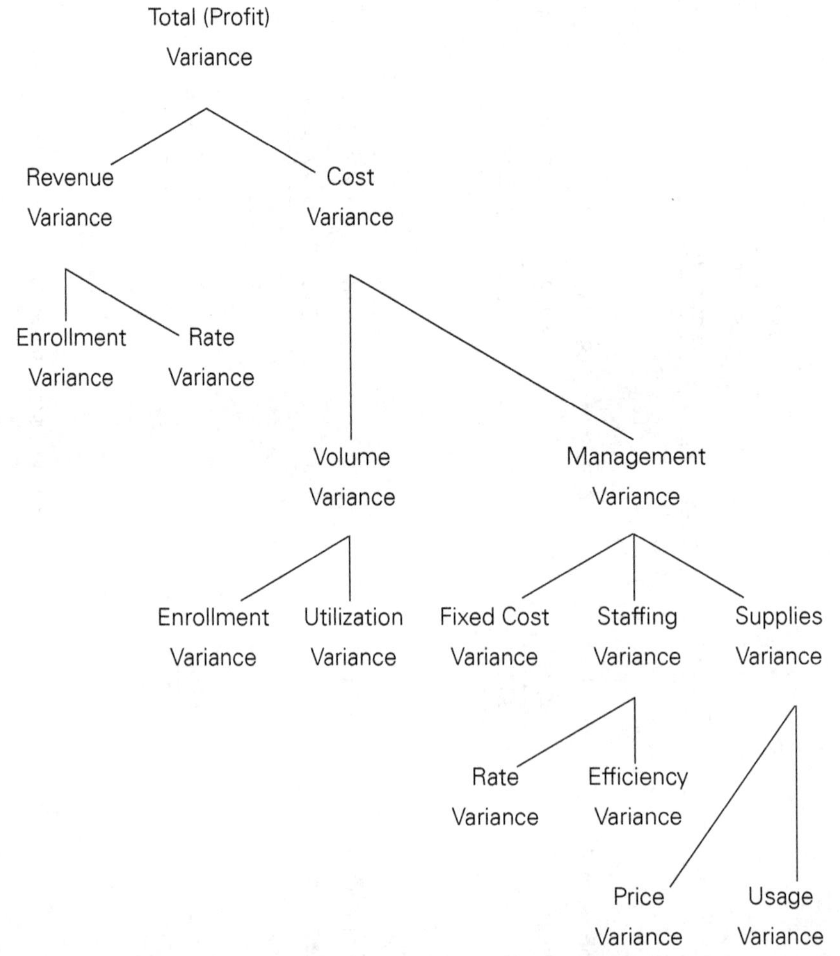

Hint: This exhibit format might be useful for presenting your numerical results.

EXHIBIT 10.6
Generic Equation List

Total variance	= Actual profit – Static profit
Revenue variance	= Actual revenue – Static revenue
Enrollment variance	= Flexible (enrollment) revenue – Static revenue
Rate variance	= Actual revenue – Flexible (enrollment) revenue
Cost variance	= Static costs – Actual costs
Volume variance	= Static costs – Flexible (enrollment/utilization) costs
Enrollment variance	= Static costs – Flexible (enrollment) costs
Utilization variance	= Flexible (enrollment) costs – Flexible (enrollment/utilization) costs
Management variance	= Flexible (enrollment/utilization) costs – Actual costs
Fixed cost variance	= Actual fixed costs – Flexible fixed costs
Staffing variance	= Actual staffing costs – Flexible (enrollment/utilization) staffing costs
Rate variance	= (Static hourly labor rate – Actual hourly labor rate) x Actual number of hours per episode x Actual utilization rate x Actual enrollment
Efficiency variance	= (Expected number of hours per episode – Actual number of hours per episode) x Expected hourly labor rate x Actual utilization rate x Actual enrollment
Supplies variance	= Flexible (enrollment/utilization) supplies costs – Actual supplies costs
Price variance	= (Static price – Actual price) x Actual units
Usage variance	= (Flexible units – Actual units) x Static price

Note: Not all of the above equations are necessarily useful to all product lines.

CASE 11

CENTURY OAKS HEALTH

BUDGETING CONCEPTS

Century Oaks Health (COH) is a large health system with services spanning a wide area of North Carolina. Chestnut Physician Practice (CPP) is the multispecialty physician group within COH. COH is the market leader across the region, with Brookberry Medical Center (BMC) as its primary competitor. In one particular city—Klein, North Carolina—BMC has primary market share. Klein General Hospital (KGH) is the local hospital.

KGH owns an outpatient clinic building, which is located close to the hospital. BMC is currently leasing the building and providing specialty care in the outpatient setting as well as inpatient consult services. Ancillary volumes at KGH have declined, and more procedures are provided at BMC's outpatient location. But KGH is ending the lease with BMC as of December 31, 2021, because it is unhappy with BMC's services. In the past year, BMC response times to inpatient needs have declined, which has increased hospital length of stay and negatively affected patient satisfaction.

You are the chief operating officer (COO) for CPP. Colleen Kim, president of KGH, has contacted your colleague, Byron Richardson, vice president for strategy and business development at COH, to discuss the possibility of CPP providing more services in Klein. In late October 2021, they are discussing CPP taking over the lease of the outpatient location and providing inpatient consultations as well as professional reads for the KGH specialty needs. Colleen requests that this turnover occur on January 1, 2022.

Because you are the physician practice's COO, Byron is requesting your input on financial and operational recommendations. You must decide whether to proceed with this outreach opportunity and persuade your CEO and executive team colleagues to follow your recommendation. Specifically, you need buy-in from CPP's leadership team, which will be operating the new site. Their initial feedback includes concerns regarding the quick turnaround to meet KGH's expectations. In addition, they are concerned that you have overcommitted with unrealistic promises of a budget that would meet CPP and COH expectations. They are accustomed to a monthly financial review process and are concerned about the sustainability of this location, especially if no ancillaries are provided there.

You share your vision with your team at CPP as you charge them with completing the due diligence that will inform your presentation to the CPP and COH executive teams. You request that your team return with insights to build a budget for the first six months as well as an annual budget projected after start-up. This site will fall under your operational oversight, so you want to understand the potential financial impact of future years before recommending the new site.

Given the proposed January 1 launch, approval is needed within two weeks. Your team returns with the following information, along with the information in the case 11 spreadsheet. Because your financial analyst position is currently vacant and your team is in the midst of another large project, you decide to personally create the budget from your team's input to inform your recommendations.

Providers

Based on local population as well as operational model needs, you and your team recommend two providers for the site; a specialist is needed when the site opens, and an advanced practice provider (APP) should be hired after three months. Provider compensation is estimated based on benchmarks, with the specialist's total compensation at $425,000 annually and the APP's compensation at $120,000 annually. Physician benefits are estimated at 18 percent and APP benefits at 21 percent.

Clinic Operations

The ambulatory leader shared the following information based on a similar outreach site for the same specialty care area:

- The clinic business hours are five days per week, with two clinic sessions per day.

- Physician clinics: The specialist is in ambulatory clinic 4.5 hours each weekday and sees 2.5 patients each hour. Within the first six months, 70 percent of the physician clinic visits are anticipated to be new patient visits (NPVs) while 30 percent are anticipated to be return patient visits (RPVs). After the first six months, the percentages of NPVs and RPVs remain the same, but the clinic's efficiency is anticipated to increase, leading to 3 patient visits per hour.
- APP clinics: The APP is in clinic six hours each weekday, with 2.5 patients per hour. Of the APP clinic visits, 10 percent are anticipated to be NPVs while 90 percent are anticipated to be RPVs.
- Anticipated staffing needs (all staffing benefits are estimated at 21 percent; estimated salaries are based on the midpoint of the position):
  - Clinic coordinator to be leader of this site as well as other current outreach sites. Their benefits will be at 50 percent shared expense to this site. (Full-time equivalent [FTE] midpoint: $70,000)
  - Clinical support specialist for registration, scheduling, and preauthorizations as well as other administrative support. This is a higher position than front desk staff. Future incremental hires may be lower-cost positions. (FTE midpoint: $40,000)
  - Certified medical assistant for clinical intake, patient phone needs, backup of clinical support specialist, and other clinical support. This person is hired at a higher level than a certified nursing assistant because they support the preauthorization process and provide other support backup. (FTE midpoint: $36,000)
- Start-up and ongoing operational clinic expenses are included in the case 11 spreadsheet. All expenses have been estimated based on similar outreach sites. The president of KGH shared that the lease of the new site is $16 per square foot, and there are 3,800 square feet. There are a potential of 12 exam rooms, but only 6 will be needed for the two providers.

Inpatient Operations

The revenue cycle team shared information that can be applied to the anticipated collections from inpatient operations. Based on your conversations with KGH, you understand the inpatient scope and anticipated provider effort/time investment. For other sites, you have recommended a provider service agreement. However, for this site, you recommend that CPP bill the professional fees for the inpatient services provided. This aligns with KGH's leadership vision as well.

- The specialty physician provides consultation services at the hospital each weekday morning. Based on discussions between COH and KGH, there is potential for a contract to include weekend and after-hours coverage.
- The physician rounds on patients five days a week and allocates 2.5 hours a day to consults. You anticipate two consults per hour. Patients are on hospitalist service while in the hospital.
- The physician will read imaging studies for KGH. These are in addition to the operational model, and you anticipate covering the physician's compensation for this activity with minimal additional revenue.

Revenue

Previous revenue trends (collections per Current Procedural Terminology [CPT] code) within this specialty at a similar site were used to project revenue for the site. Data trends provided are specific to professional billing in a non-provider-based clinic, as this reflects the new Klein site. Every CPT code used for billing has a certain number of corresponding work relative value units (RVUs). The report contains work RVUs per CPT as well as historical total collections per CPT (exhibit 11.1). The work RVUs represent the relative level of time, skill, training, and intensity needed to provide a given service. To project anticipated clinic revenue, it is recommended that you average payment per NPV or RPV and apply to projected volumes. This can be a simple average or weighted average. For consult revenues, you can also apply average payment per consult to projected volumes to determine revenue.

Management has asked you to build a revenue model that links the assumptions above to anticipated revenue during (1) the first six months (assume 18 business weeks after clinic opens), and (2) annually after the first six months (assume 48 business weeks).

EXHIBIT 11.1
Work Relative Value Units (RVUs) Supportive Data for Projected Revenue Calculation

New Patient Visits (NPVs): Clinic

CPT Code	*Office Visit NPV Level Description*	*Work RVUs*	*Collections*
99201	Level I	0.45	$ 35.46
99202	Level II	0.88	54.16
99203	Level III	1.34	99.30
99204	Level IV	2.30	154.63
99205	Level V	3.00	188.36

Return Patient Visits (RPVs): Clinic

CPT Code	*RPV Level Description*	*Work RVUs*	*Collections*
99211	Level I	0.17	$ 3.03
99212	Level II	0.45	30.45
99213	Level III	0.92	57.59
99214	Level IV	1.42	89.00
99215	Level V	2.00	124.51

Inpatient Consults (ICs)

CPT Code	*IC Level Description*	*Work RVUs*	*Collections*
99251	Level I	1.00	$ 94.61
99252	Level II	1.50	118.57
99253	Level III	2.27	135.28
99254	Level IV	3.25	189.43
99255	Level V	4.00	224.85

PART V

FINANCIAL MANAGEMENT CONCEPTS

CASE 12

GULF SHORES SURGERY CENTERS

TIME VALUE ANALYSIS

Gary Hudson was born and raised in Pensacola, Florida. He obtained his bachelor's degree in business from Florida State University, where he enrolled in the Naval Reserve Officers Training Corps program. After graduation, he received a commission in the US Marine Corps. Following his release from active duty, Gary used his GI Bill benefits to obtain a master's degree in health services administration from the University of Florida. His first job in healthcare was as a special projects coordinator/financial analyst at a large Miami hospital. He enjoyed his work there, but his ultimate goal was to return to Pensacola as the manager of a small healthcare business, where he would have more responsibility and authority. After five years in Miami, Gary became the chief operating and financial officer of Gulf Shores Surgery Centers, an investor-owned chain of ambulatory surgery centers with six locations in Florida's Panhandle.

Immediately after assuming his new position, Gary found himself facing several decisions. First, Gary had to select a bank or banks to meet the financial needs of Gulf Shores. He has approached two local banks—Sun Trust and BankSouth—about the interest rates they offer on a savings account and a certificate of deposit (CD) as well as the rate charged on a term loan. Sun Trust and BankSouth offer the same interest rate on each financial product and only differ in the frequency of compounding (exhibit 12.1).

Second, a wealthy patient was so impressed with the care she received at Gulf Shores that she decided to make a series of donations to the facility. She will donate \$75,000 a year for the first six years (t = 1 through t = 6, where t = time) and \$150,000 annually for the following six years (t = 7 through t = 12). The first deposit will be made a year from today (t = 1). In addition, she has just written a check for $250,000, which Gary will invest immediately ($t = 0$). Gary will invest all the donations in a CD as they become available. CDs are generally offered in maturities of 6 months to 10 years, and interest can be handled in one of two ways: the investor (buyer) can receive periodic interest payments, or the interest can automatically be reinvested in the CD. In the latter case, the buyer receives no interest during the life of the CD but receives the accumulated interest plus the principal amount at maturity. Because the goal of this investment is to accumulate funds for future use, as opposed to generating current income, all interest earned on the CD would be reinvested.

Third, Gulf Shores may launch substantial building renovations. In this circumstance, it would be forced to borrow $250,000 from a bank. Gary is considering two options for a term loan:

1. A five-year term loan that would be repaid in equal annual installments, with the first payment due at the end of Year 1. Gary hopes to pay off the loan early—at the end of Year 3.
2. A seven-year loan that would be repaid in annual installments of differing amounts, with the first payment due at the end of Year 1. For the first three years of the loan, the annual installment would be projected cash surpluses ($25,000 at the end of Year 1, $50,000 at the end of Year 2, and $75,000 at the end of Year 3). For the final four years of the loan, the annual installment would be a fixed (but currently unspecified) cash flow, X, at the end of each year from Year 4 through Year 7.

Finally, Gulf Shores has a board-designated building fund to pay for projected facility renovations starting in eight years and lasting for four years (at $t = 8, 9, 10$, and 11). Current building renovation costs are estimated to be $14,500,000 a year, but they are expected to increase at a rate of 3.5 percent a year. So far, Gulf Shores has accumulated $15,000,000 (at $t = 0$). Gary's long-term financial plan is to add $5,000,000 in each of the next four years (at $t = 1, 2, 3$, and 4). Then, he plans to make equal annual contributions in each of the following three years ($t = 5, 6$, and 7).

All the decisions Gary faces involve time value analysis.

EXHIBIT 12.1
Interest Rates on Three Financial Products

Bank	*Product*	*Compounding*	*Nominal Interest Rate*
Sun Trust	Savings account	Weekly	2.0%
	Certificate of deposit	Monthly	3.0
	Term loan	Quarterly	4.0
BankSouth	Savings account	Daily	2.0%
	Certificate of deposit	Annually	3.0
	Term loan	Semiannually	4.0

CASE 13

MID-ATLANTIC SPECIALTY, INC.

FINANCIAL RISK

Mid-Atlantic Specialty, Inc., is a not-for-profit corporation formed by physicians in the College of Medicine at Mid-Atlantic University. Mid-Atlantic, with more than 600 physicians, provides the medical staff for University Hospital. In addition, Mid-Atlantic staffs and administers a network of 25 ambulatory care clinics and centers at 10 locations within 50 miles of University Hospital. In 2017, Mid-Atlantic generated more than $500 million in revenues from about 40,000 inpatient stays and 750,000 outpatient visits.

Christina Chen, chief financial officer, manages several investment portfolios that Mid-Atlantic has established, primarily to provide capital for clinical services that use expensive diagnostic and treatment equipment. Christina is currently considering the creation of a new investment fund that will have an initial balance of $10 million. She has identified 10 stocks for Mid-Atlantic to consider:

- *DaVita Inc.* provides kidney dialysis services through a network of 2,664 outpatient dialysis centers in the United States, serving 202,700 patients, and 241 outpatient dialysis centers in other countries.
- *Amgen Inc.* (formerly Applied Molecular Genetics Inc.) is an American multinational biopharmaceutical company headquartered in Thousand Oaks, California.
- *Laboratory Corporation of America Holdings* is headquartered in Burlington, North Carolina, and operates one of the largest

clinical laboratory networks in the world, with a US network of 36 primary laboratories.
- *McKesson Corporation* is an American company distributing pharmaceuticals and providing health information technology, medical supplies, and care management tools.
- *Humana Inc.* is a for-profit American health insurance company based in Louisville, Kentucky.
- *Medtronic plc* is the world's largest medical device company, operating in 140 countries and employing more than 86,000 people.
- *Pfizer Inc.* is an American multinational corporation headquartered in New York City and one of the world's largest pharmaceutical companies.
- *Anthem, Inc.*, is a provider of health insurance in the United States. It the largest for-profit managed health care company in the Blue Cross Blue Shield Association, with approximately 40 million members.
- *UnitedHealth Group Incorporated* is an American for-profit managed health care company based in Minnetonka, Minnesota, and is the largest healthcare company in the world by revenue.
- *Centene Corporation* is a large publicly traded company and a multiline managed care enterprise that serves as a major intermediary for both government-sponsored and privately insured healthcare programs.

Christina has obtained 1/1/2020 forecasted adjusted closing prices on the 10 stocks from Hudson and Allen, the investment adviser used by Mid-Atlantic, and these appear in exhibit 13.1. Hudson and Allen also provided 2015–2018 monthly returns on the 10 stocks and the S&P 500 (see case 12 spreadsheet). Finally, Hudson and Allen forecasted a 3 percent rate of return on 1-year T-bills (the risk-free rate) and a 6 percent rate of return on the S&P 500 (the market portfolio). With this information, Christina can start to prepare her analysis of the risk and required return of the 10 stocks. She is also concerned about recent political events that may affect the risk of the investment portfolio. More specifically, an international conflict has resulted in an increase in the price of oil, and this has sparked concern about future inflation. In addition, substantial change to the tax code could be implemented by Congress and this uncertainty has caused investors to become more risk averse.

EXHIBIT 13.1
1/1/2020 Forecasted Adjusted* Closing Prices on 10 Stocks

Investment	*Symbol*	*1/1/2020 Forecasted Adjusted Closing Prices*
DaVita Inc.	DVA	$ 60.72
Amgen Inc.	AMGN	195.08
Laboratory Corporation of America Holdings	LH	148.12
McKesson Corporation	MCK	135.15
Humana Inc.	HUM	325.99
Medtronic plc	MDT	92.27
Pfizer Inc.	PFE	43.77
Anthem, Inc.	ANTM	317.89
UnitedHealth Group Incorporated	UNH	281.58
Centene Corporation	CNC	68.46

*Adjusted for dividends paid by a stock during 2019.

PART VI

CAPITAL ACQUISITION

CASE

14

PACIFIC HEALTHCARE (A)

BOND VALUATION

Pacific Healthcare is an investor-owned hospital chain that owns and operates nine hospitals in Washington, Oregon, and Northern California. Marcia Long, a recent graduate of a prominent health services administration program, has just been hired by Washington Medical Center, Pacific's largest hospital. Like all new management personnel, Marcia must undergo three months of intensive training at the system level before joining the hospital.

Marcia began her training in January 2021. Her first assignment at Pacific was to review its latest annual report. This was a stroke of luck for Marcia because her father owned several bonds issued by Pacific, and she was especially interested in whether her father had made a good investment. To glean more information about the bonds, she examined Note E to Pacific's consolidated financial statements, which lists the company's long-term debt obligations, including its first-mortgage bonds, installment contracts, and term loans. Exhibit 14.1 contains information on four of the first-mortgage bonds listed in Pacific's annual report. All four bonds pay interest semiannually. (For more information on bond ratings, see Standard & Poor's website at www.standardandpoors.com or the Moody's Investors Service website at www.moodys.com.)

Pacific's chief financial officer, Hugo Welsh, found out about Marcia's interest in the firm's debt financing. "Because you are so interested in our financial structure," he said, "I want you to do the bond valuation and make a presentation to our executive committee." Hugo then asked Marcia to perform the calculations required to complete exhibit 14.2 and to think about some of the questions that members of the committee might ask her about the numbers.

EXHIBIT 14.1
Pacific Healthcare: Long-Term Bonds

Face Amount	*Current Price*	*Par Value*	*Coupon Rate*	*Years to Maturity*	*Bond Rating*
$ 48,000,000	$ 800.00	$1,000	4.50 %	5	A+
32,000,000	865.49	1,000	8.25	15	A+
100,000,000	1,220.00	1,000	12.625	25	A+
64,000,000	747.48	1,000	7.375	25	A+

EXHIBIT 14.2
Pacific Healthcare: Long-Term Bond Stated (Nominal) Yields

Face Amount	*Annual Yield to Maturity*	*2022 Coupon Payments*	*2022 Current Yield*	*1/1/2023 Expected Price*	*2022 Capital Gain Yield*	*2022 Total Yield*
$ 48,000,000						
32,000,000						
100,000,000						
64,000,000						

CASE

15

SENIOR CARE ENTERPRISES

BOND REFUNDING

SENIOR CARE ENTERPRISES, a leading provider of post-acute healthcare, is a for-profit corporation that operates more than 500 skilled nursing facilities, 30 assisted living centers, 150 outpatient rehabilitation therapy clinics, and 50 hospice and home care centers. Aram Catalan, the financial vice president of Senior Care, is reviewing the minutes of the company's final 2021 board of directors meeting. The major topic discussed at the meeting was whether Senior Care should refund any of its currently outstanding bond issues. Of particular interest is a $100 million, 30-year bond issue sold approximately five years ago and carrying an 8.0 percent coupon rate. Several of the board members had taken markedly different positions on the question. At the conclusion of the meeting, the chair of the board asked Aram to prepare a report analyzing the alternative points of view.

The bonds in question, which are rated single A, were issued in January 2017 when interest rates were higher than they are today. Issuing the bonds at the time was necessary because Senior Care needed the capital to expand its rehabilitation services business line. Now, five years later, with lower rates, Senior Care can sell A-rated bonds that carry a lower interest rate than that set on the 2017 issue.

Because Aram wants to have flexibility regarding when the 2017 issue could be retired, he insists that the bonds be made callable after five years. In general, during the first few years when a call is permitted, a call premium is equal to one year's interest and gradually declines as the current date approaches the maturity date. At maturity, the call premium is zero. The Senior Care bonds can be called on January 1, 2022 (the end of Year 5), but an initial call premium of one year's interest payment—$80 per $1,000 par value bond—would have to be paid. This premium declines by 8.0% ÷ 25 = 0.32 percentage points, or $3.20, each year. Thus, if the bonds were called on January 1, 2027 (the end of Year 10), the call premium would be (8.0% ÷ 25) × 20 = 6.4%, or $64, where 20 represents the number of years remaining to maturity. The flotation cost on this issue is 1.5 percent of the face amount, or $1,500,000. Senior Care's federal-plus-state tax rate is 30 percent. If the bonds had not been callable, Senior Care would have had to pay an interest rate of only 7.3 percent, 70 basis points less than the actual 8.0 percent coupon rate.

Aram estimates that Senior Care could currently sell a new issue of 25-year A-rated bonds at an interest rate of 7.0 percent. The call of the old and sale of the new bonds could take place five to seven weeks after the decision to refund has been made; this time is required to give legal notice to bondholders and arrange the financing needed to redeem the current issue. The flotation cost of the refunding issue would be 1 percent of the new issue's face amount, and funds from the new issue would be available from the underwriters the day they are needed to pay off the old bonds. Aram had proposed at the last board of directors' meeting that Senior Care call the 8.0 percent bonds at the first opportunity and replace them with a new, lower coupon rate issue. Although the refunding cost would be substantial, he believed the interest savings of 100 basis points per year for 25 years on a $100 million issue would be well worth the cost. He had not anticipated adverse reactions from any of the board members; however, three of them voiced strong reservations about his refunding proposal.

The first director was Pamela Mathias, a long-term member of Senior Care's board and chair of Mathias & Company, an investment banking house that caters primarily to institutional clients such as insurance companies and pension funds. She argued that calling the bonds for refunding would not be well received by the major institutions that hold Senior Care's outstanding bonds. According to Pamela, the institutional investors who hold the bonds purchased them on the expectation of receiving the 8.0 percent interest rate for at least 10 years, and these investors would be very unhappy if a call occurred after only 5 years. Because most of the leading institutions hold some of Senior Care's bonds and because the firm typically sells new bonds to finance its growth every four or five years, it would be most unfortunate if institutional investors developed a feeling of ill will toward the company.

The second director was Vincent Marchiano, who is a relatively new member of the board and president of a local bank. He also opposed the call, but for an entirely different reason. He believed that the decline in interest rates was not yet over, saying that a study by his bank suggested that the long-term interest rate on A-rated corporate bonds might fall to 6.8 percent next year. Under questioning from the other board members, however, Vincent admitted that the interest rate decline could be over and that interest rates might remain at 7.0 percent or even increase to 7.2 percent. When pressed, he produced the following probability distribution that his bank's economists had developed for interest rates on A-rated corporate bonds one year from now (January 1, 2023):

Probability	*Interest Rate on A-Rated Corporate Bonds*
0.1	6.4%
0.2	6.6
0.4	6.8
0.2	7.0
0.1	7.2

The board agreed that any analysis of the impact of prospective interest rates on the refunding decision would assume that Senior Care would issue a 24-year bond if the refunding occurred one year hence.

The third director who opposed the call, Kim Mitchell, had a lot of questions and wanted to fully understand all the risks and returns before making a decision. She noted that interest rates had been quite volatile lately and that if rates rose before the new issue could be sold but after Senior Care had committed to the refunding, the refunding would be a disaster. Therefore, she wondered how much interest rates could increase before Senior Care lost on the refunding. Indeed, the sensitivity of the refunding net present value to current interest rate levels would be a valuable tool in making the refunding decision. Another issue Kim thought was of consequence to the refunding decision was tax rates. Senior Care's marginal tax rate could fall from its current value of 30 percent. Understanding the relationship between the attractiveness of refunding and the firm's tax rate would be useful. Such an analysis could also show if the refunding decision is affected by ownership (for-profit versus not-for-profit) status.

As Aram's assistant, you have been asked to perform the bond refunding analysis and to report your conclusions and recommendations at the next executive committee meeting. With the model at hand, you begin your work, noting that, for ease of calculation, the model assumes annual coupons.

CASE 16

PACIFIC HEALTHCARE (B)

STOCK VALUATION

Pacific Healthcare is an investor-owned hospital chain that owns and operates nine hospitals in Washington, Oregon, and Northern California. Marcia Long, a recent graduate of a prominent health services administration program, has just been hired by Washington Medical Center, Pacific's largest hospital. Like all new management personnel, Marcia must undergo three months of intensive training at the system level before joining the hospital.

In Case 14, Marcia conducted an analysis of Pacific's bonds and presented her findings to the company's executive committee. Pacific's chief financial officer, Hugo Welsh, was very impressed with the quality of her presentation. Furthermore, other members of the committee stated that they learned a great deal about debt financing from the presentation and would like to see a similar presentation on equity financing. Because Marcia would be leaving corporate headquarters to start her hospital assignment in less than four weeks, Hugo immediately assigned her the task of analyzing Pacific's equity situation and preparing another presentation for the executive committee.

Marcia began by reexamining Pacific's annual report to get some basic financial data. Then, she searched Yahoo! Finance (http://finance.yahoo.com), CNN Business (www.cnn.com/business), Bloomberg (www.bloomberg.com), and MSN Money (http://money.msn.com) for current market data as well as analysts' forecasts for Pacific Healthcare and the market. She discovered that Pacific's stock is currently (December 31, 2021) selling for $8 per share, current dividend is $0.480 per share (paid on December 31, 2021), and beta coefficient is 1.2. In addition, she learned that the yield on long-term Treasury bonds is 5 percent and that a market return of 11 percent is expected. Most analysts forecast that Pacific will grow about 10 percent per year for the next five years (2022–2026) and 4 percent per year thereafter (2027 and beyond). Based on these growth forecasts, she assembled the forecast dividends per share, as shown in exhibit 16.1.

Hugo asked Marcia to focus on the current value of Pacific's stock and whether it is undervalued or overvalued, the expected stock price over the next five years, and the expected dividend yield and capital gains yield over the next five years. He also suggested that Marcia consider the possible questions members of the committee might ask about the numbers.

EXHIBIT 16.1
Pacific Healthcare: Historical and Forecast Dividends per Share

	Year	*Dividends per Share*
Historical	2016	$0.215
	2017	0.324
	2018	0.353
	2019	0.362
	2020	0.391
	2021	0.480
Forecast	2022	$0.528
	2023	0.581
	2024	0.639
	2025	0.703
	2026	0.773
	2027	0.804
	2028	0.836

CASE 17

SEATTLE CANCER CENTER

LEASING DECISIONS

Seattle Cancer Center is a nationally known not-for-profit inpatient and outpatient facility dedicated to the prevention and treatment of cancer. Specific treatment services include surgery, chemotherapy, bone marrow transplantation, radiation therapy, and photodynamic therapy.

For the past 10 years, Seattle has been working diligently to perfect noninvasive brain surgery techniques. One technique, Gamma Knife radiosurgery, was developed in the 1950s and 1960s by Dr. Lars Leksell, a prominent Swedish neurosurgeon. The first patient treatment site was opened in 1968 in Stockholm, Sweden, while the first site in the United States was established in Pittsburgh, Pennsylvania, in 1977.

The Gamma Knife uses 201 separate radiation sources to treat certain brain cancers. Each radiation beam is weak and hence does not damage normal brain tissue, but when the separate beams are focused on a single point by a collimator helmet, the equipment delivers a dosage sufficient to be highly effective. The Gamma Knife is especially useful in the treatment of arteriovenous malformations, but it can also be used to treat certain types of benign tumors and even some small malignant lesions. The primary clinical benefit of the procedure is the significant reduction in the risk associated with traditional surgical procedures, in which the morbidity and mortality rates are substantial, especially for patients with deep lesions. In addition to treating cancer, it can treat functional disorders such as Parkinson's disease tremors and the pain that results from trigeminal neuralgia. (For more information about the Gamma Knife, including an informative video on Gamma Knife surgery, see the manufacturer's website at http://gammaknife.com.)

The procedure calls for a team approach, including a neurosurgeon, radiation physicist, radiologist, and radiation therapist. The neurosurgeon selects the patients appropriate for the procedure and performs the stereotactic process required to localize the target area. The radiation physicist works with a computer program to calculate the appropriate dosimetry, while the radiologist performs a computed tomography scan, a magnetic resonance imaging scan, an angiogram, or a combination of the three to help the neurosurgeon localize the lesion.

The dosimetry calculations are especially complex. Because differing thicknesses of skull and brain will attenuate the beams to varying degrees, the amount of radiation applied is highly dependent on where the lesion is located and the size and shape of the patient's skull. The actual application of the radiation takes between 20 minutes and 2 hours, and the patient is generally released after only a short period of observation.

Seattle plans to acquire a new Gamma Knife to replace its current model. The equipment has an invoice price of $3 million, including delivery and installation charges, and it falls into the MACRS (modified accelerated cost recovery system) five-year class, with current allowances of 0.20 in Year 1, 0.32 in Year 2, 0.19 in Year 3, 0.12 in Year 4, 0.11 in Year 5, and 0.06 in Year 6. The manufacturer of the equipment will provide a maintenance contract for $100,000 per year, payable at the beginning of each year, if Seattle buys the equipment. Furthermore, the purchase could be financed by a four-year, simple-interest, conventional (taxable) bank note that would carry an interest rate of 9 percent.

Regardless of whether the equipment is purchased or leased, Seattle's managers do not think the new Gamma Knife will be used for more than four years, at which time Seattle plans to open a new radiation therapy facility. Land on which to construct a larger facility has already been acquired, and the building should be ready for occupancy at that time. The new facility is designed to enable Seattle to use several new radiosurgery procedures. Thus, the Gamma Knife replacement is viewed as a "bridge," to serve only until the new facility is ready. The expected physical life of the equipment is 10 years, but medical equipment of this nature is subject to unpredictable technological obsolescence.

After considerable debate among Seattle's managers, they concluded that there is a 25 percent probability that the residual (salvage) value after four years will be $800,000; a 50 percent probability that it will be $1.2 million; and a 25 percent probability that it will be $1.6 million, which makes the residual value quite risky. If the residual value is judged to have high risk, any risk analysis would add a 4-percentage-point adjustment to the base discount rate used in the base case lease analysis to obtain the appropriate rate for the residual value.

GB Financing, a leasing company that is partially owned by the Gamma Knife manufacturer, has presented an initial offer for Seattle to lease the equipment for annual payments of $675,000, with the first payment due on delivery and installation and subsequent payments due at the beginning of each succeeding year of the four-year lease term. This rental price includes a service contract under which the equipment would be maintained in good working order. GB Financing would buy the equipment from the manufacturer under the same terms that were offered to Seattle, and GB Financing would have to enter into a maintenance contract with the manufacturer for $100,000 per year. (For more information on leasing healthcare equipment, see the CSI Leasing website at www.csileasing.com/solutions/healthcare-equipment-leasing/.)

Unlike Seattle, GB Financing forecasts a $1.6 million residual value. Its estimate is based on the following facts:

- There is no technology on the horizon that would make the Gamma Knife obsolete.
- The Gamma Knife has a physical life estimated to be two and a half times longer than the four-year lease term.
- GB Financing is more skilled than Seattle in selling used equipment, especially the Gamma Knife.

GB Financing's federal-plus-state tax rate is 30 percent, and, if the lease is not written, it could invest the funds in a four-year term loan of similar risk yielding 8 percent before taxes.

Randall Rhee Williams, Seattle's chief financial officer, has the final say on all the firm's lease-versus-purchase decisions, but the actual analysis of the relevant data will be conducted by Seattle's capital funds manager, Vanessa Seagle. In the past, Randall and Vanessa have agreed on analytical methodologies, but in discussing this lease analysis, they ended up in a heated discussion about the appropriate discount rate to use in the analysis.

Randall argued that the cash flows associated with performing stereotactic radiosurgery are very uncertain. He is convinced that payers are not going to be nearly as generous in the future as they have been in the past in reimbursing for such procedures, so the revenue stream is highly speculative. Accordingly, he thinks that a high discount rate should be used in the analysis. Vanessa, on the other hand, believes that leasing is a substitute for "other financing," which is a blend of debt and equity capital. Consequently, she asserts that the lease-analysis cash flows should be discounted at Seattle's corporate cost of capital, 10 percent. However, it is possible that both Randall and Vanessa are wrong.

Both Randall and Vanessa believe that lessees should not blindly accept the first offer made by potential lessors but should conduct a complete analysis from the viewpoint of both parties and then, using this knowledge, negotiate the best deal possible. Thus, knowing the range of lease payments that is acceptable to both parties is important.

There is a possibility that Seattle will move to its new radiation facility earlier than anticipated and hence before the expiration of the lease. Furthermore, if the neurosurgeon—the primary user of the Gamma Knife—leaves the staff and is not immediately replaced, the equipment would be useless. Thus, Randall is considering asking GB Financing to include a cancellation clause in the lease contract. Under such a clause, Seattle would be able to return the equipment at any time during the lease term after giving a minimum 30-day notice. Before negotiations begin, Seattle must assess the impact of such a clause on the riskiness of the lease to both parties and any consequences the clause might have on the terms of the lease.

In addition, Randall is aware that many lessors are now writing per-procedure leases, in which the lease payment is tied to the number of procedures performed rather than a fixed amount. He wonders what the consequences would be for both the lessee and the lessor if a per-procedure lease were used instead of a conventional lease. GB Financing has quoted a per-procedure lease rate of $7,000 for an expected annual volume of 100 procedures. However, previous experience at Seattle indicates that volume could easily be as low as 70 procedures or as high as 130 procedures. Considering current charges and reimbursement rates, Seattle expects to realize a net revenue per procedure of roughly $10,000.

Seattle's leadership has discussed obtaining tax-exempt financing for the Gamma Knife should it be purchased. If it is purchased, the cost of tax-exempt (municipal) debt would be only 5 percent. To complicate matters, Seattle currently has more than $5 million in excess funds invested in marketable securities earning 3 percent. These funds, rather than debt financing, could be used to purchase the equipment.

GB Financing would probably obtain a $1.5 million simple-interest loan to leverage the lease. The terms of this loan have not been finalized, but the bank has indicated that the interest rate would be in the range of 7 to 9 percent. Such leveraging could affect GB Financing's ability to negotiate lease payments, so understanding the impact of leveraging from the lessor's perspective is important.

You were hired as a consultant to recommend a course of action for the Gamma Knife acquisition. Prepare a report that addresses all the issues raised by the parties involved and that makes a final recommendation regarding the acquisition.

PART

COST OF CAPITAL AND CAPITAL STRUCTURE

VII

CASE 18

SOUTHEASTERN HOMECARE

COST OF CAPITAL

Southeastern Homecare was founded in 1992 in Miami, Florida, as a taxable partnership by Maria Gonzalez, MD; Ramon Garcia, RN; and Ron Sparks, LPT. Its purpose is to provide an at-home alternative to hospitals and ambulatory care facilities for basic healthcare services provided by physicians, registered nurses, licensed practical nurses, and physical therapists. (For more information on home health services, see the website of the National Association for Home Care & Hospice at www.nahc.org.)

Southeastern enjoyed enormous success from the first day of operations. Even its founders were surprised at how easy it was to establish and run the business. Its founding coincided with the search by third-party payers for alternative and potentially less costly delivery settings. Because of its success in metropolitan Miami, Southeastern expanded services into Fort Lauderdale and West Palm Beach and then moved into other metropolitan areas in Florida and across the US Southeast. Southeastern also expanded services at each location to include occupational, speech, and rehabilitation therapies.

The founders had personal resources sufficient to start Southeastern, and they had enough confidence in their business plan to commit most of their own funds to the new venture. However, after only six years, the external capital requirements brought on by rapid growth exhausted the founders' personal funds, forcing them to borrow heavily. Soon, although they still needed external capital to finance growth, their ability to borrow at reasonable rates was exhausted. Thus, in 2002, the founders incorporated Southeastern and, in 2005, sold common stock to the public through an initial public offering. Today, the founders still retain a large but minority ownership position at Southeastern, and the Southeastern stock trades in the over-the-counter market.

Southeastern is widely recognized as one of the regional leaders in the home health care industry. In 2016, it won an award for being one of the 100 best-managed small companies in the United States. It has two operating divisions: Healthcare Services and Information Systems. The Healthcare Services division operates the home health care services at all 22 locations. Because sales and earnings in this division are relatively predictable, the business risk of this division is about average.

The Information Systems division maintains the computer software that Southeastern designed to control its own operations and sells it to other home health care companies. This software integrates inventory control, visit scheduling, clinical record keeping, billing and collections, and payroll into a single package. Although the software is excellent, it competes head-to-head with platforms by several major software firms as well as with those of other information system services and information management consulting firms. Because of this competition and the rapid technological changes in the information services field, Southeastern considers the Information Systems division to carry more business risk than the Healthcare Services division.

Although its growth has been exceptional, Southeastern developed on a more random than planned basis. The founders simply decided on a location for a new facility, ran an advertisement in a local newspaper to hire clinical professionals and support staff, sent an experienced manager from an established office to the new location, and began to make money almost immediately. Formal decision structures were almost nonexistent, but Southeastern's head start and bright, energetic founders easily overcame any deficiencies in managerial decision-making processes.

However, recent changes in the market for home health care services portend a more difficult environment in the future. First, relatively generous Medicare payments before the Affordable Care Act payment reform provisions started in 2014 produced intense competition in the home health care industry. Other investor-owned home health care agencies sprang up quickly, especially in major cities, and several hospitals in Southeastern's service area, including not-for-profits, began to offer home health care services. Second, the rapid increase in home care expenditures prompted payers to drastically reduce reimbursement amounts just as new capacity emerged. In particular, the Centers for Medicare & Medicaid Services has reduced payment rates made under the home health prospective payment system for several years in a row.

Because of these changes, Southeastern's board of directors concluded that the company must start to apply state-of-the-art techniques in both its operations and its corporate managerial processes. As a first step, the board directed the financial vice president (VP) to develop an estimate for Southeastern's cost of capital. The financial VP, in turn, directed Southeastern's treasurer, Clark Ruffin, to prepare and submit a cost-of-capital estimate in two weeks. Clark has an accounting background, and his primary task since taking over as treasurer has been cash and short-term liability management. Thus, he is somewhat apprehensive about his new assignment, an apprehension that is heightened by the fact that one board member is a well-regarded University of Florida finance professor.

Clark began by reviewing Southeastern's 2021 financial statements (presented in exhibit 18.1 in simplified form) and by obtaining some selected market data (presented in exhibit 18.2). Next, he assembled the following data.

Long-Term Debt

- Southeastern's long-term debt consists of 7.5 percent coupon, BBB-rated, semiannual payment bonds with 15 years remaining to maturity. The bonds recently traded at a price of $956.31 per $1,000 par value bond. The bonds are callable in five years at par value plus a call premium of $50, for a total of $1,050.
- The founders have an aversion to short-term debt, so such debt is used only to fund cyclical working capital needs. Southeastern's financial plan calls for the issue of 30-year bonds to meet long-term debt needs.

Equity

- Southeastern's last dividend (D0) was $0.17, and its common stock now sells at a price of $5.25 per share. The company has 10 million common shares outstanding.
- In the past few years, Southeastern has averaged a 20 percent return on equity and has paid out about 50 percent of its net income as dividends.
- Southeastern's historical beta, as measured by several analysts who follow the stock, falls in the range of 1.3 to 1.5.

Capital Structure

- Southeastern's federal-plus-state tax rate is 30 percent.
- Southeastern's target capital structure includes weights of 35 percent long-term debt and 65 percent common stock.

Operating Divisions

- About 60 percent of Southeastern's operating assets are used by the Healthcare Services division, and 40 percent by the Information Systems division. Management's best estimate of the Healthcare Services division's beta is 1.0.
- Following are the two divisions' investment opportunities for next year:

Healthcare Services Division	*Estimated internal rate of return*
A new office in Naples, Florida	9.3%
A new office in Sarasota, Florida	9.8%
Information Systems Division	*Estimated internal rate of return*
A new healthcare record system	12.2%
Expanded billing software	13.2%

Clark has hired you as a consultant to develop Southeastern's overall corporate cost of capital. You will have to meet with the financial VP—and possibly with the president and the full board of directors (including the founders and the finance professor)—to present your findings and answer any questions.

In addition to performing a standard analysis, you must address several concerns raised at the last board meeting about the cost-of-capital estimate. First, the board chair noted that the corporate cost-of-capital estimate is influenced by several factors, some of which are external to the business. She is particularly interested in the impact on the estimated corporate cost of capital of factors that cannot be influenced by managerial actions.

Second, the divisional presidents questioned why a single cost of capital will be applied across the company, regardless of any divisional risk differences. Clark has asked you to address this question by developing divisional costs of capital.

Third, the founders alerted the group to the threat posed by home health care businesses started by not-for-profit hospitals, which have both cost (in the sense that they do not pay dividends) and tax advantages. To help assess this threat, Clark has asked you to estimate the cost of capital for an average not-for-profit hospital's home health care business, starting with the information in exhibit 18.3.

Finally, one board director is worried about the difference between the target capital structure and the current structure as reported on the balance sheet. Clark wondered if this should be a matter for consideration.

EXHIBIT 18.1
Southeastern Homecare: 2021 Financial Statement Extracts (in Millions of Dollars)

Balance Sheet

Cash and marketable securities	$ 2.5	Accounts payable	$ 1.1
Accounts receivable	5.9	Accruals	1.0
Inventory	1.3	Notes payable	0.2
Current assets	$ 9.7	Current liabilities	$ 2.3
Net fixed assets	41.9	Long-term debt	20.0
		Common stock	29.3
Total assets	$51.6	Total liabilities	$51.6

Income Statement

Net revenues	$80.6
Cash expenses	71.8
Depreciation	2.8
Taxable income	$ 6.0
Taxes	2.4
Net income	$ 3.6
Dividends	1.8
Additions to retained earnings	$ 1.8

EXHIBIT 18.2
Selected Market Data

Expected Rate of Return on the Market

Expected rate of return on the S&P 500 Index = 11.0%

Required Rate of Return on Long-Term Debt of an Average Company

Yield on A-rated long-term debt for a company with a beta of 1.0 = 7.0%

Current Yield Curve on US Treasury Securities

Term to Maturity	*Yield*
3 months	2.5%
6 months	3.0
9 months	3.3
1 year	3.5
5 years	4.0
10 years	4.5
15 years	4.8
20 years	5.0
25 years	5.1
30 years	5.2

EXHIBIT 18.3
Selected Not-for-Profit Hospital Data

Average Long-Term Capital Structure

30% debt

70% equity (net assets)

Average Cost of Debt

Interest rate on A-rated tax-exempt bonds = 5.0%

CASE 19

RN TEMPS, INC.

CAPITAL STRUCTURE ANALYSIS

RN Temps, Inc., franchises "rent-a-nurse" businesses to independent operators throughout the United States. The concept of the business is the same as that of other temporary staffing services, such as Manpower and Kelly Services, except that RN Temps deals only with registered nurses. (For an example of a company similar to RN Temps, Inc., see www.interimhealthcare.com.)

The rationale for developing RN Temps is as follows:

- *Many healthcare providers, especially hospitals, have difficulty hiring and retaining nurses, so nursing professionals are almost always in high demand.* Traditionally, hospitals have been the dominant employer of nurses, employing almost 60 percent of the roughly 2.7 million working nurses in the United States. Today, nurses have opportunities that did not exist even just half a century ago, such as in the nurse practitioner, nurse anesthetist, and critical care or neonatal specialist professions. In addition, they can work in home health agencies, nursing homes, utilization review departments, physicians' offices or outpatient surgery centers, and a multitude of other nonhospital settings such as schools. Of all the work settings, hospitals are generally considered to be the least desirable because of the hard work, rigid work conditions, and irregular working hours associated with them.
- *Providers generally want to minimize fixed costs, so any staffing requirements that may not be permanent are often filled by temporary workers.* In addition, when vacancies occur among permanent

workers, providers often need temporary nurses to carry the load until the vacancies are filled with permanent personnel.

- *Although nursing salaries have increased over the past 10 years, real wages have barely kept up with inflation.* Furthermore, a large number of nurses have quit the profession for a variety of reasons, including family responsibilities. Many of these nurses are willing to work occasionally but not on a permanent basis. About one in five nurses works part time.
- *Typically, the nurses who want to work on a selective basis have spouses who provide family coverage health insurance.* These nurses do not require extensive fringe benefits, such as pension plans or paid vacations, and because they are part-time workers, they are not eligible for unemployment insurance or workers' compensation. Thus, if the average fringe-benefit package paid for permanent nurses is, say, 25 percent of salary, a temporary services company could offer its nurses a salary that is 5 percent higher than the salary provided by traditional employers; could "rent out" the nurses at 5 percent less than it costs providers to hire permanent nurses, including all fringe benefits; and could pocket what remains of the 15 percent spread after administrative costs are paid. Note, however, that the actual rates charged by RN Temps franchisees are related more to local supply-and-demand conditions than to costs.

Franchisees buy the exclusive right from RN Temps, Inc., the franchisor, to use the RN Temps name within a specified territory. In addition, franchisees receive marketing and management support from RN Temps as well as the right to lease computers and other office equipment under relatively favorable terms. Finally, franchisees can purchase expendable office supplies directly from RN Temps at substantial savings from retail prices.

To start operations, a franchisee recruits a pool of nurses from the local labor market. Then, when a client needs a temporary nurse, the local manager matches the client's specific needs with a qualified nurse from the pool. The bill for services is sent to the client by the franchisee according to the number of hours—verified by a time card—the nurse works for the client. The client has no responsibility for the nurse's salary or fringe benefits, which are all handled by the RN Temps franchisee.

Tiffany Radcliff, a registered nurse from Albuquerque, New Mexico, who left the profession to get an MBA from the University of New Mexico, founded RN Temps in 1990. The firm grew rapidly from its base in Albuquerque, first by expanding operations into different cities across the Southwest and then by franchising into other parts of the country. Tiffany was a devout believer in the virtues of equity financing. RN Temps had issued debt periodically, especially to finance company-owned business expansion, but Tiffany always used the firm's free cash flow to retire the debt as soon as possible. Recent growth has involved franchising, in which the franchisee puts up the required capital, and hence there has been no need for outside capital for several years.

Tiffany believes that RN Temps's high-growth days are over. First, numerous companies that offer competing services have appeared on the scene. Second, the number of hospitals, which are the primary clients, has declined over the years since RN Temps was founded, and a meaningful increase in hospital beds is unlikely in the foreseeable future. Third, many hospitals have created flexible staffing pools for nurses, which, for all practical purposes, are in-house temporary work agencies. Finally, many large employers of nurses are recruiting internationally, which lessens the demand to find temporary workers domestically. Thus, Tiffany expects RN Temps's earnings to grow relatively slowly in the future.

Tiffany's financial manager, Paul Duncan, has been suggesting for years that RN Temps should use some debt in its capital structure. "After all," says Paul, "everybody else uses debt, and some of our competitors use more than 50 percent debt financing. Also, an under-leveraged company is exposed to a hostile takeover because raiders can use the firm's excess debt capacity to finance the bid."

If RN Temps were to recapitalize, the borrowed funds would be used to repurchase stock in the open market, as the funds are not needed to grow the business. Tiffany's reaction to Paul's prodding is cautious, but she is willing to give Paul the chance to prove his point. Paul has worked with Tiffany for the past six years and knows that the only way he can convince her that RN Temps should use debt financing is to conduct a comprehensive capital structure analysis.

On the basis of previous conversations, Paul knows that Tiffany has four major concerns about debt financing: (1) its impact on the firm's return on equity (ROE) as reported in the firm's financial statements, (2) its impact on the firm's stock price and corporate cost of capital (CCC), (3) the financial effects of potential changes in business risk of RN Temps, and (4) whether industry averages have any implications for the level of debt financing of RN Temps.

Impact of Financial Leverage on ROE

RN Temps has 20 million shares of common stock outstanding, which are traded in the over-the-counter market. The current share price is $1.50, so the total market value of the firm's equity is $30 million. The book value of equity is also $30 million, so the stock now sells at its book value. The firm's federal-plus-state tax rate is 30 percent. Tiffany owns 20 percent of the outstanding stock, and others in the management group own an additional 10 percent.

Although RN Temps's earnings before interest and taxes (EBIT) are expected to be $6 million next year, there is some uncertainty in the estimate, as indicated by the following probability distribution:

Probability	*EBIT*
0.25	$5,000,000
0.50	6,000,000
0.25	7,000,000

To address Tiffany's first concern, Paul plans to construct partial income statements (beginning with EBIT) for four levels of debt as measured by the book value total-debt-to-total-assets ratio: zero, 25 percent, 50 percent, and 75 percent. For this analysis, which will not be used to make the actual capital structure decision, Paul intends to use a cost of debt of 10 percent regardless of the amount of debt financing used. Furthermore, any risk implications to stockholders must be identified.

Impact of Financial Leverage on Stock Price and CCC

To address Tiffany's second concern, Paul used a technique to value zero-growth firms at different debt levels. Clearly, the results of this analysis do not apply exactly to RN Temps, which is expected to experience slow growth, as opposed to zero growth, over the coming years. Here are the equations used in the analysis:

$$E = \{EBIT - [R(R_d) \times D]\}(1 - T)/R(R_e)$$

$$V = E + D$$

$$P = (V - D_0)/n_0$$

$$n_1 = n_0 - D/P$$

where

E = market value of equity

EBIT = earnings before interest and taxes

$R(R_d)$ = cost of debt

D = market (and book) value of new debt

D_0 = market value of old debt

T = tax rate

$R(R_e)$ = cost of equity

V = total market value

P = stock price after recapitalization

n_0 = number of shares before recapitalization

n_1 = number of shares after recapitalization

Paul arranged for a meeting with an investment banker who specializes in corporate financing for service companies. After several hours, the pair agreed on the estimates for the relationships between the use of debt financing and RN Temps's capital costs, which are shown in exhibit 19.1. Finally, Paul obtained industry capitalization data for companies that franchise professional services along with the matching debt ratings on the basis of rough guidance given by S&P Global Ratings (www.spglobal.com/ratings/en/). These data are provided in exhibit 19.2.

Business Risk and Industry Averages

Tiffany's third concern is potential changes in the healthcare industry and how they might affect the basic business risk of RN Temps should they occur. To address this concern, Paul produced exhibit 19.3, which contains the estimated cost of debt and equity at different amounts of debt financing if there is an increase in business risk. Note that the values in exhibit 19.3 are for the purposes of what-if analysis only. The best current estimates of the financing costs at alternative debt levels are given in exhibit 19.1.

Tiffany's final concern is whether industry averages have any implications for the level of debt financing of RN Temps. Paul uncovered the following additional industry data: The average healthcare franchise business has (1) a debt ratio of 40 percent, (2) a times interest earned (TIE = EBIT/annual interest payment) ratio of 4.0, and (3) cash and marketable securities on hand equal to 70 percent of its annual interest payment. RN Temps has cash and marketable securities on hand of $900,000.

Paul knows that Tiffany is familiar with capital structure theory and will want to know the value of the firm according to the Modigliani-Miller model with corporate taxes and the Miller model. To ease comparisons, Paul assumes that the value of RN Temps, with zero debt financing, is $30 million in both models. He also assumes that the personal tax rates are 15 percent on stock income and 35 percent on debt income.

Put yourself in Paul's shoes and convince Tiffany that the business should use debt financing.

Amount Borrowed	*Cost of Debt*	*Cost of Equity*
$ 0	—	14.0%
5,000,000	9.0%	14.3
10,000,000	9.5	15.0
15,000,000	10.5	16.0
20,000,000	12.5	17.5

EXHIBIT 19.1
RN Temps, Inc.: Estimated Cost of Debt and Equity at Different Amounts of Debt Financing

Percentile	*Debt Ratio*	*Debt Rating*
10th	10%	AAA
25th	25	AA
40th	35	A
Median	40	BBB
60th	55	BB
75th	65	B
90th	72	C

EXHIBIT 19.2
Healthcare Franchise Industry Data: Debt Ratings at Different Levels of Debt Ratio (Total Debt to Total Assets)

Amount Borrowed	*Cost of Debt*	*Cost of Equity*
$ 0	—	15.0%
5,000,000	10.0%	15.5
10,000,000	11.0	16.5
15,000,000	13.0	18.0
20,000,000	16.0	20.0

EXHIBIT 19.3
RN Temps, Inc.: Estimated Cost of Debt and Equity at Different Amounts of Debt Financing if Increase in Business Risk

PART VIII

CAPITAL ALLOCATION

CASE 20

JONES MEMORIAL HOSPITAL

CAPITAL BUDGETING DECISION CRITERIA

Jones Memorial Hospital (JMH) is an 800-bed, acute care, for-profit teaching hospital affiliated with one of the largest private universities in the United States. In addition to serving the primary and secondary clinical care needs of the neighboring population, JMH serves as a tertiary and quaternary referral center for the entire region. For the most part, referred patients seek specialty care that requires unique and often costly clinical expertise and treatment that is available only at select institutions. Thus, it is not surprising that specialty care programs provide JMH with about 75 percent of its net operating income.

The Functional GI and Motility Disorders (FGID) Clinic at JMH is the premier site, both nationally and internationally, for referral of patients with functional GI and motility disorders. The FGID Clinic's multidisciplinary, patient-centered approach integrates medical, physiological, and psychological factors in the evaluation, understanding, and treatment of patients with these disorders. The FGID Clinic also serves as a leading tertiary referral site for patients who have difficult-to-diagnose illnesses or challenging disease or disorder management issues.

FGID Clinic providers include three gastroenterologists, one physician assistant, and one nurse. On some afternoons, the FGID Clinic is also staffed with a fellow (gastroenterologist in training), who is supervised by an attending physician. The FGID Clinic's gastroenterologists are also routinely involved with consulting on patients at JMH with severe functional GI or motility disorders and with physicians who call for advice regarding their patients. The FGID Clinic often has visiting gastroenterologists and trainees from other states and countries who are interested in learning more about the clinical approach, diagnosis, and treatment of patients with functional GI and motility disorders and want to improve their interviewing and patient skills.

A key clinical service of the FGID Clinic is the GI Motility Laboratory (Motility Lab) that was established by Dr. Carl Forsyth. The Motility Lab provides comprehensive diagnostic evaluation and advice on management of patients with a variety of GI motility disorders, including:

- Diagnostic anorectal motility tests for fecal incontinence, constipation, or rectal pain
- Ambulatory pH and impedance testing
- Esophageal motility testing
- Hydrogen breath tests for small bowel bacterial overgrowth and carbohydrate malabsorption
- Breath tests for *Helicobacter pylori* infection
- Motility wireless capsule (SmartPill) testing of gastric, small bowel, colonic, and whole gut transit
- Biofeedback treatment for fecal incontinence, constipation, or rectal pain

Patients with GI motility disorders are seen initially in the FGID Clinic or the Hospital Esophageal Clinic, or they may be referred directly to the Motility Lab for diagnostic motility testing and advice on further management. Diagnostic motility tests may be scheduled directly by outside physicians, but the Motility Lab usually receives a medical consultation from one of the clinicians affiliated with the FGID Clinic.

Although the Motility Lab generates less than 10 percent of the FGID Clinic's total net patient service revenue, it is a vital component. The Motility Lab currently performs 600 motility tests per year. In recent years, the number of referrals to the Motility Lab has increased dramatically, primarily because of the FGID Clinic's reputation for state-of-the-art patient care. Dr. Forsyth believes there is a need for expanded laboratory capacity because some patients are being referred to other providers to ensure timely testing. In addition, Dr. Forsyth recently said in a senior management team meeting, "The motility laboratory is poised to grow as the level of diagnostic sophistication in gastroenterology continues to advance. Disorders of GI motility and functional GI disorders will comprise a larger percentage of GI practice in the future, not only in hospitals but in the offices of gastroenterologists.

I estimate that a new lab would have a volume of 600 motility tests in the first year and increase at an annual rate of 10 percent thereafter." These factors have prompted the FGID Clinic's administrative director, Edith Hargrove, to seek immediate approval for the addition of a second motility laboratory.

To begin the capital expenditure request process, Edith is currently reviewing quotes from various manufacturers of equipment for a motility laboratory. Her research on quality and cost has narrowed the field of competing manufacturers to one: Digestive Diagnostics, Inc. The motility laboratory equipment, computers, blood pressure and pulse oximeter machines, and other necessary equipment are estimated to cost $300,000, with installation costs of $30,000. The equipment falls into the MACRS (modified accelerated cost recovery system) five-year recovery period, which has annual recovery allowances of 20 percent, 32 percent, 19 percent, 12 percent, 11 percent, and 6 percent. The Internal Revenue Service defines depreciable basis as the purchase price of the assets plus any transportation and installation costs.

Edith thinks that the payer mix, average charge per test, and average allowances, discounts, and bad debt of the second motility laboratory will be the same as the Motility Lab, and these data are shown in Exhibit 20.1. One source of concern to her is the recent slowing of increases in payment rates for GI services at the same time as operating costs continue to grow. To be conservative, Edith estimates that average net patient revenue per test for the second motility laboratory will increase at an average annual rate of 2 percent over the next five years.

The largest operating cost of the second motility laboratory will be labor, as it will require a dedicated full-time GI motility nurse to perform the appropriate testing. A nurse from the hospital's endoscopy laboratory who has salary and benefits costing around $100,000 per year has been identified for the full-time position. He will be sufficient staffing until test volume reaches 750 patients, at which point another full-time nurse will be hired at the same salary and benefits. There is a shortage of GI motility nurses, which will likely result in higher-than-average increases in salaries and benefits as hospitals compete for this specialized staffing; Edith estimates this will be 5 percent per year or more for the foreseeable future.

The space for the second motility laboratory will be rented and Edith has two options. The Smith medical office building adjacent to JMH can provide basic clinic space at a cost of $3,250 per month with no increase over the next five years. Alternatively, Edith has been approached by Omega Healthcare REIT, a local real estate investment trust company that owns, operates, and finances medical clinics and offices. Omega Healthcare can provide the necessary space for $3,000 per month for the next two years and $3,500 per month for three years after that.

Maintenance of the equipment is important and regular biomedical engineering inspection and service are essential to ensure test fidelity. A local firm has agreed to provide regular maintenance service for $50,000 per year. Catheters, disposable linen, and other supplies cost $20 per test. Edith estimates that maintenance and supply cost per test will increase by 3 percent per year over the next five years.

The FDIG Clinic recently disposed of some five-year-old motility laboratory equipment, and Edith uses the information from that to estimate an equipment salvage value of $100,000 at the end of five years. The risk-adjusted pretax project cost of capital for the second motility laboratory is 8 percent, and JMH has a tax rate of 21 percent.

Edith has every expectation that the new motility laboratory will succeed and operate over the full five-year period. However, if the anticipated volume does not materialize, payment rates are less than expected, or costs are higher than predicted, it may be best to abandon the second motility laboratory prior to the end of the five-year period. This would involve selling the equipment and reassigning staff, along with other expenses. Edith estimates that termination of the second motility laboratory would have a net abandonment value of $300,000 at the end of Year 1, $250,000 at the end of Year 2, $200,000 at the end of Year 3, and $100,000 at the end of Year 4.

Edith has asked you to create a capital budgeting model to help her decide whether JMH should invest in a second motility laboratory. For the purpose of simplicity, Edith asks you to assume annual cash flows.

EXHIBIT 20.1
Payer Mix; Average Charge per Test; and Average Allowances, Discounts, and Bad Debt of Motility Lab Tests

Payer	*Payer Mix*	*Average Charge per Test*	*Contractual Allowances, Discounts, and Bad Debts as a Percentage of Charges*
Medicare	41%	$ 900	40%
Medicaid	17	700	35
Blue Cross/private insurance	17	1,000	50
Managed care	14	800	45
Self-pay	5	500	90
Other	6	800	30

CASE 21

CORAL BAY HOSPITAL

TRADITIONAL PROJECT ANALYSIS

Coral Bay Hospital is a 250-bed, investor-owned hospital located in Coral Bay, Florida, which is known as the Sport Fishing Capital of the World. The hospital was founded in 1946 by Dr. Rob Winslow, a prominent Florida physician, on his return from service in World War II. He relinquished control of Coral Bay in 1967 while it was still small and in a relatively quiet setting. However, in recent years, South Florida has experienced a population explosion, which has fostered high economic growth and the need for more healthcare services. Today, under a succession of excellent CEOs, Coral Bay is recognized as one of the leading healthcare providers in the area.

Coral Bay's management is currently evaluating a proposed ambulatory surgery center (ASC). (For more information on ambulatory surgery, see the Ambulatory Surgery Center Association website at www.ascassociation.org.) More than 80 percent of all outpatient surgery is performed by specialists in gastroenterology, gynecology, ophthalmology, otolaryngology, orthopedics, plastic surgery, and urology. Ambulatory surgery requires an average of about one and a half hours to complete; minor procedures take about one hour or less, and major procedures typically take two or more hours. About 60 percent of the procedures are performed under general anesthesia, 30 percent under local anesthesia, and 10 percent under regional or spinal anesthesia. In general, operating rooms are built in pairs so that a patient can be prepped in one room while the surgeon is completing a procedure in the other room.

The outpatient surgery market has experienced significant growth since the first ASC opened in 1970. By 1990, about 2.5 million procedures were being performed at stand-alone ASCs, and by 2021, the number had grown to more than 25 million. This growth has been fueled primarily by three factors. First, rapid advancements in technology have enabled many procedures that were historically performed in inpatient surgical suites to be offered in outpatient settings. This shift was caused mainly by advances in laser, laparoscopic, endoscopic, and arthroscopic technologies. Second, Medicare has been aggressive in approving new minimally invasive surgery techniques, so the number of Medicare patients using outpatient surgery services has grown substantially. Third, patients prefer outpatient surgeries because they are more convenient, and third-party payers prefer them because they are less costly.

Because of these factors, the number of inpatient surgeries has remained more or less flat over the past 20 years, whereas the number of outpatient procedures has continuously grown more than 10 percent annually. Rapid growth in the number of outpatient surgeries has been accompanied by a corresponding growth in the number of outpatient facilities nationwide. The number currently stands at about 5,300, so competition in many areas has become intense. Somewhat surprisingly, no ASC exists in Coral Bay's immediate service area.

Coral Bay currently owns a parcel of land adjacent to its facility that is a perfect location for the ASC. The hospital bought the land five years ago for $300,000, and this amount is reported as an asset on the balance sheet. Last year, $50,000 was spent to clear the land and put in sewer and utility lines, and this amount was reported as an operating expense on the hospital's income statement and tax return last year (and thus not included in the asset value of the land on the balance sheet). If sold in today's market, the land would bring in $400,000, net of all fees, commissions, and taxes. Land prices have been extremely volatile, so Coral Bay's standard procedure is to assume a salvage value equal to the current value of the land. Of course, land is not depreciated for either book or tax purposes.

The ASC building, which would house four operating suites, would cost $15 million, and the equipment would cost an additional $5 million, for a total of $20 million. Assume that both the building and the equipment fall into the MACRS (modified accelerated cost recovery system) five-year class for tax depreciation purposes. (In reality, the building would have to be depreciated over a much longer period than the equipment.) The project will probably have a long life, but Coral Bay typically assumes a five-year life in its capital budgeting analyses and then approximates the value of the cash flows beyond Year 5 by including a terminal, or salvage, value in the analysis. To estimate the salvage value, Coral Bay typically uses the market value of the building and equipment after five years, which for this project is estimated to be $12 million before taxes, excluding the land value. (Note that taxes must be paid on the difference between an asset's salvage value and its tax book value at termination. For example, if an asset that cost $10,000 has been depreciated down to $5,000 and then sold for $7,000, the firm owes taxes on the $2,000 excess in salvage value over tax book value.)

The expected volume at the ASC is 20 procedures a day. The average charge per procedure is expected to be $3,000, but charity care, bad debts, managed care plan discounts, and other allowances lower the net patient revenue amount to $2,000. The ASC would be open 5 days a week, 50 weeks a year, for a total of 250 days a year. Labor costs to run the ASC are estimated at $3,200,000 per year, including fringe benefits. Utilities, including hazardous waste disposal, would add another $100,000 in annual costs.

If the ASC were built, the hospital's cash overhead costs would increase by $72,000 annually, primarily for housekeeping and buildings and grounds maintenance. In addition, the ASC would be allocated $50,000 of Coral Bay's current $2.8 million in administrative overhead costs. On average, each procedure would require $400 in expendable medical supplies, including anesthetics. Although Coral Bay's inventories and receivables would increase slightly if the center is constructed, its accruals and payables would also increase. The overall change in net working capital is expected to be small and hence not material to the analysis. Coral Bay's marginal federal-plus-state tax rate is 30 percent.

When the project was mentioned briefly at the last medical staff meeting, several questions were raised. Coral Bay's chief of medicine expressed concern over the impact of the ASC on the current volume of inpatient surgeries. This concern prompted an analysis by the head of the surgery department, who reported that an ASC could siphon off up to $2 million in inpatient cash revenues annually. When pressed, the department head estimated that such a reduction in volume could also lead to a $1 million reduction in annual cash expenses.

The CEO has asked DeShawn Williams, Coral Bay's director of capital budgeting, to undertake a complete project analysis. DeShawn was invited to the last board of directors' meeting, where several concerns about the proposed ASC were raised by board members. The first concern was the impact of potential inflation on project profitability. Both input costs and charges in the healthcare industry have been rising at about twice the rate of overall inflation. Furthermore, inflationary pressures have been highly variable. For the proposed ASC, DeShawn assumes constant inflation rates of 3 percent for costs (except depreciation) and 2 percent for net patient revenue. In previous capital budgeting decisions, DeShawn assessed the impact of uncertain future inflation on project profitability with a table such as the one shown in exhibit 21.1.

The second concern identified at the last board of directors' meeting was the impact on profitability if actual outcomes differ from the expected ones. Recently, the board was forced to close a day care center that appeared to be profitable when analyzed two years ago but turned out to be a big money loser. The board does not want a repeat of that occurrence. One of the directors stated that she thought Coral Bay was putting too much faith in the numbers. "After all," she pointed out, "that is what got us into trouble on the day care center. We need to start worrying more about how projects fit into our strategic vision and how they affect the services we currently offer."

To address the second concern, sensitivity, scenario, and break-even analyses are an integral component of the risk analysis that DeShawn will present to the board. The data needed for the risk analysis were obtained from the department heads of surgery, marketing, and facilities. Three input variables were identified as highly uncertain:

- *Number of procedures per day*. If another entity enters the local ASC market, the number of procedures could be as low as 16 per day. Conversely, if acceptance is strong and no competing ASCs are built, the number of procedures could be as high as 22 per day, compared with the most likely value of 20 per day.
- *Average net patient revenue per procedure*. The most likely amount of $2,000 per procedure is a function of the types of procedures performed and the amount of managed care penetration. If surgery severity were high (i.e., if a higher number of complicated procedures than anticipated were performed) and managed care penetration remained low, then the average amount per procedure could be as high as $2,200. Conversely, if the severity were lower than expected and managed care penetration increases, the average amount per procedure could be as low as $1,800.
- *Building and equipment salvage value*. If real estate and medical equipment values stay strong, the building and equipment salvage

value could be as high as $14 million, but if the market weakens, the salvage value could be as low as $10 million, compared with a most likely value of $12 million.

DeShawn estimates that the probabilities of the worst case, most likely case, and best case scenarios are 25 percent, 50 percent, and 25 percent, respectively.

DeShawn consulted with Sophia Garcia, Coral Bay's chief financial officer, about both the risk inherent in the hospital's average project and how the hospital typically adjusts for risk. Sophia told DeShawn that historical scenario-analysis data show that the average project has a coefficient of variation of net present value in the range of 3.5 to 4.0. If a proposed project has an estimated coefficient of variation above this range, it is judged to be high risk and 3 percentage points are added to the 7 percent corporate cost of capital to adjust for higher project risk. Since the board was forced to close a day care center two years ago, the board has insisted on this adjustment for projects judged to be high risk and has consistently rejected unprofitable projects that have used the risk-adjusted corporate cost of capital.

The final concern raised at the last board of directors' meeting was the consequences of doing nothing. More specifically, what if a competitor uses an ASC to lure the hospital's surgeons away? What if the hospital's surgeons leave to develop an ASC on their own? One director believes that a missed opportunity for such a venture could precipitate a severe reduction in the hospital's surgical volume by disenfranchising busy and productive surgeons and polarizing the medical staff. The ASC may be a way of preserving the surgeons' volume, attracting new surgeons, retaining productive surgeons, and growing market share and geographic penetration. However, it is also possible that some surgeons, such as those who will not be able to participate in the ASC because of their surgical specialty or safe harbor compliance, may not support the project.

Produce a complete project analysis on the ASC. What should DeShawn recommend to the board of directors?

EXHIBIT 21.1
Impact of Uncertain Future Inflation on NPV of Proposed Ambulatory Surgery Center

		Level of Net Patient Revenue Inflation						
		0%	1%	2%	3%	4%	5%	6%
	0%	NPV	NPV	NPV	NPV	NPV	NPV	NPV
Level of	1%	NPV	NPV	NPV	NPV	NPV	NPV	NPV
Cost	2%	NPV	NPV	NPV	NPV	NPV	NPV	NPV
Inflation	3%	NPV	NPV	NPV	NPV	NPV	NPV	NPV
	4%	NPV	NPV	NPV	NPV	NPV	NPV	NPV
	5%	NPV	NPV	NPV	NPV	NPV	NPV	NPV
	6%	NPV	NPV	NPV	NPV	NPV	NPV	NPV

NPV: net present value

CASE 22

NATIONAL REHABILITATION CENTERS

STAGED-ENTRY ANALYSIS

National Rehabilitation Centers (NRC) is one of the nation's leading providers of outpatient rehabilitative medicine. It was founded in 1988 in Phoenix, Arizona, by a group of five individuals who recognized the need for cost-effective alternatives to traditional hospital-based rehabilitative services. This vision has become the hallmark of NRC, which continues to provide the highest-quality, most cost-effective care available. (For more information on rehabilitative medicine, see the American Academy of Physical Medicine and Rehabilitation website at www.aapmr.org.)

To keep the costs of rehabilitative services low, NRC uses the latest in noninvasive treatment procedures, which reduces direct costs and results in quicker recoveries. In addition, the company encourages patients to begin aggressive rehabilitation as early as possible, which helps them return to normal functioning more quickly than under conventional treatment protocols. In spite of NRC's relatively short history, its strategy has worked wonders, and it quickly expanded from a local to a regional to a national company. Today, NRC is a multibillion-dollar publicly traded company with nearly 750 locations in all 50 states, Puerto Rico, the United Kingdom, and Australia.

For several years, NRC's board of directors has been considering expanding its service line to include sports medicine. The American College of Sports Medicine defines this field as the physiological, biomechanical, psychological, and pathological phenomena associated with exercise and sports. (For more information on sports medicine, see the American College of Sports Medicine website at http://acsm.org.) Because rehabilitative and sports medicine services have much in common, expansion into this rapidly growing area of healthcare seems natural.

NRC's board is examining two proposals related to the expansion. Proposal A involves a single, large investment that would immediately give the company a national presence in sports medicine. In essence, all the current rehabilitation facilities deemed suitable to offer sports medicine services would be renovated, equipped, and staffed as required to offer sports medicine services. The amount of capital investment at each earmarked location would vary significantly, but the average cost is estimated at about $800,000 per facility. With roughly 500 locations identified as being suitable for the sports medicine service line, the estimated cost of Proposal A is in the vicinity of $400 million. Although the profitability analysis of Proposal A is only preliminary, its internal rate of return is thought to be in the range of 20 to 25 percent.

Proposal B, on the other hand, involves a more deliberate, two-stage approach to the expansion. Stage 1 of Proposal B calls for a trial program in which only one of NRC's nine regions would offer sports medicine services. If the results of Stage 1 meet the company's profit targets, Stage 2, which calls for the expansion of sports medicine services into the remaining eight regions, would be implemented.

Proposal A requires a much larger capital investment than does Stage 1 of Proposal B. However, overall, Proposal B is more costly than Proposal A, even when the time value of money is considered, because Proposal A's large up-front investment leads to greater efficiencies in contracting, construction, recruitment, and marketing. In spite of Proposal A's cost advantage, several board members are concerned about the wisdom of Proposal A because it requires a large investment in a service line that is new to NRC. Other board members, however, see no difference between rehabilitation and sports medicine services; one board member even said, "Healthcare is healthcare."

The primary task at hand now is to evaluate Proposal B, which includes the trial program and possible expansion into all regions. To date, NRC has spent $7 million to develop a sports medicine concept that matches its approach to rehabilitative medicine. Of the $7 million, $2 million has been expensed for tax purposes, and the remaining $5 million has been capitalized and will be amortized over the five-year operating life of Stage 1. According to a specific Internal Revenue Service ruling requested by NRC, if neither Proposal A nor B is implemented, the $5 million could be immediately expensed.

If NRC decides to go ahead with Stage 1, it would immediately spend $2 million to perform local labor-market studies to ensure that the locations identified for the sports medicine program could be staffed. The next step would be to buy the land needed at locations where totally new facilities are required. In total, land acquisition costs, which are assumed to occur at the end of Year 1, are expected to be $10 million. New construction and renovations at the chosen locations would take place during Year 2 and Year 3, and equipment would be installed during the last quarter of Year 3. Additional personnel would be hired as needed at the end of Year 3. The total amount required for new buildings, renovations to existing buildings, and equipment (plus a relatively small amount for recruitment) is estimated to be $50 million. For planning purposes, half this amount is assumed to be spent at the end of Year 2 and the other half at the end of Year 3.

Any new buildings would fall into the MACRS (modified accelerated cost recovery system) 39-year tax depreciation class for tax purposes, but (for simplicity) both the buildings and equipment needed are assumed to fall into the MACRS 7-year class. Appropriate depreciation allowances are given in exhibit 22.1. NRC would begin to depreciate the buildings and equipment during Year 4, the year in which the trial sports medicine program would be initiated. The trial program would be evaluated at the beginning of Year 6. If the results are satisfactory, the program would be expanded to the other eight regions. If the program does not meet expectations, it would be terminated at the end of Year 8. If terminated, the land would have an estimated market value of $10 million at that time, and the buildings and equipment would have a market value of $30 million.

NRC's marketing department has projected two demand scenarios for Stage 1. If demand for the sports medicine program is poor, total revenues are forecasted to be $40 million for Year 4, the first year of operations. However, if demand is good, revenues are expected to be $60 million. At this point, the best guess is that there is a 50 percent chance of poor demand and a 50 percent chance of good demand. If demand is good, revenues are expected to increase by 6 percent each year after Year 4. If demand is poor, revenue growth is expected to be only 3 percent.

In terms of operating costs, variable costs are expected to be 30 percent of revenues. Fixed costs (other than depreciation), which are expected to total $25 million in Year 4, are forecasted to increase after the initial year of operations at the anticipated overall rate of inflation, 2 percent.

If the board approves Stage 2, NRC would spend an additional $480 million on land, buildings, and equipment to expand into the other eight regions. This expenditure would be evenly split between Year 6 and Year 7.

As shown in the following table, the net cash inflows forecasted for Stage 2 depend on the demand scenario:

	Net Cash Flow		
End of Year	*High Demand*	*Medium Demand*	*Low Demand*
6	($240,000,000)	($240,000,000)	($240,000,000)
7	(240,000,000)	(240,000,000)	(240,000,000)
8	210,000,000	160,000,000	70,000,000
9	228,000,000	170,000,000	75,000,000
10	241,000,000	175,000,000	75,000,000
11	256,000,000	180,000,000	75,000,000
12	500,000,000	350,000,000	150,000,000

Note that the net cash flows have been "bumped up" in Year 9 to reflect the cash flows from those facilities in the test region. In addition, note that the project is expected to last beyond Year 12, and an allowance for the value of these future cash flows is embedded in the Year 12 cash flows.

The estimated probabilities of the Stage 2 demand scenarios are related to the response to the Stage 1 trial program. If acceptance is poor in Stage 1, there is a 10 percent probability that demand will be high during Stage 2, a 40 percent probability that demand will be medium, and a 50 percent probability that demand will be low. However, if acceptance during Stage 1 is good, there is a 50 percent probability that demand will be high during Stage 2, a 40 percent probability that demand will be medium, and a 10 percent probability that demand will be low. Of course, these expectations may change over time as new information becomes available. Furthermore, the actual demand scenario for Stage 2 is not expected to be known until midway through Year 8, after the program has been operational nationally for six months.

NRC's current effective income tax rate is 30 percent, and this rate is projected to remain roughly constant into the future. The firm's corporate cost of capital is 9 percent, a percentage NRC adjusts up or down by 3 percentage points to adjust for project risk. NRC defines low-risk projects as those that have a coefficient of variation (CV) of net present value of less than 0.8, average-risk projects as those that have CVs in the range of 0.8 to 1.2, and high-risk projects as those that have CVs of more than 1.2.

One of the most important advantages of staged entry is that new information will become available throughout the investment period. NRC's managers recognize the value of this feature and believe that they will have a better estimate of the Stage 2 probabilities and cash flows before making the Year 6 investment. Even if Stage 2 is undertaken, there is some possibility that the project could be abandoned at the end of Year 8 if the low-demand scenario materializes. If the project is terminated at that point, the best estimate for the Year 8 abandonment cash flow is $420 million. The uncertainty of whether abandonment would occur lies more in the politics than in the economics of the decision. In the past, NRC's managers have not been inclined to admit mistakes and cut losses, so some doubt lingers about whether the abandonment decision would be made even if it is the financially right thing to do at the time.

You have been hired as a consultant to analyze the sports medicine program and to make a recommendation to NRC's board of directors regarding the best course of action. In addition to a detailed analysis of Proposal B, you have been asked to subjectively compare the relative merits of Proposal A with those of Proposal B.

EXHIBIT 22.1
MACRS Depreciation Rates

	Recovery Year				
MACRS Class	*1*	*2*	*3*	*4*	*5*
7-year	14.3%	24.5%	17.5%	12.5%	8.9%

MACRS: modified accelerated cost recovery system

Note: For ease, these allowances were rounded to the nearest one-tenth of 1 percent. In actual applications, the allowances would not be rounded.

CASE 23

NORTHWEST SUBURBAN HEALTH SYSTEM

OUTSOURCING DECISIONS

Northwest Suburban Health System is a large not-for-profit healthcare holding company that operates both not-for-profit and for-profit subsidiaries in the northwest suburbs of Chicago, Illinois. The not-for-profit subsidiaries consist of four acute care hospitals (Des Plaines General, Arlington Heights Memorial, Palatine General, and Barrington Community) and one service company (SUPPORT). SUPPORT provides various services, such as food, laundry, and medical waste disposal, to the four hospitals. The system's single for-profit subsidiary, PROPERTIES, operates several for-profit businesses, but its primary business line is real estate development—particularly medical office buildings.

Northwest Suburban's CEO, Susan Richards, has been thinking about the system's printing situation for some time. The system has a print shop, which currently operates under SUPPORT, that provides some of the printing required by the hospitals, but it does not have the capabilities to do all the work required. As shown in exhibit 23.1, Northwest Suburban currently (2021) spends about $830,000 a year on commercial contract printing, some of which could be done in-house if the system expanded its printing capability.

Of the roughly $830,000 in total vendor contracts, about $132,000 represents graphics printing—annual reports, brochures, and other promotional material. Most of the graphics printing (about $119,000) could be moved in-house, but about 10 percent of the work (e.g., the four-color annual report) would still have to be done by outside vendors.

Conversely, only about 50 percent of the almost $700,000 in forms printing, or just under $350,000 could be moved in-house. Many of the forms require highly specialized equipment, and printing such forms in-house is only cost-effective for very large businesses. Northwest Suburban's print contracts (for both graphics and forms) with vendors increased in dollar volume by about 5 percent (2 percent volume increase and 3 percent price increase) from 2020 to 2021, and this trend is expected to continue into the foreseeable future.

In 2021, the in-house print shop handled $42,837 in hospital billings. (To avoid any potential problems with SUPPORT's not-for-profit status, the print shop currently performs work exclusively for Northwest Suburban's four not-for-profit hospitals.) The print shop bills for materials only, but because material costs represent, on average, 30 percent of commercial vendors' total billings, the shop currently does about $42,837/0.30 = $142,790 in annual work on a commercial billing basis. The equipment in the print shop has a current market value of $650,000, and the shop generates about $40,000 in annual depreciation expense for tax purposes.

To move 90 percent of the vendor graphics printing and 50 percent of the vendor forms printing in-house, Northwest Suburban would have to invest in additional printing equipment. The capital investment necessary for expansion can vary significantly, depending on whether new or used equipment is purchased, on the type of main press selected, and on whether only essential or nice-to-have equipment is purchased. Exhibit 23.2 summarizes the equipment capital investment requirements. Note that the old equipment would be retained if the print shop were expanded. The new equipment would also generate tax depreciation of about $25,000 per year, and the required delivery van would cost $2,000 a year to operate (in 2021 dollars).

The print shop is located in leased space adjacent to Des Plaines General, the largest of the four hospitals. The cost of this site is $10 per square foot per year. The print shop occupies 2,000 square feet, and hence current building costs are $20,000 in annual lease payments plus $200 per month in utilities and insurance. Unfortunately, this site cannot be expanded, and hence new space is required if the print shop is to increase its capacity. Suitable space in a good location can be leased at the same rental rate ($10 per square foot per year), but the new print shop would require 3,500 square feet, increasing the annual lease cost by $35,000 – $20,000 = $15,000. (Assume that lease payments occur at the beginning of each year.)

Furthermore, the new space would require $30,000 in initial remodeling costs and an additional $100 per month in utilities and insurance costs (in 2021 dollars). Note that all leases are negotiated for a five-year period, so lease payments are not affected by inflation, which is expected to average about 3 percent per year.

The expanded print shop would require an increase in labor costs of \$98,400; these costs are summarized in exhibit 23.3. Labor costs to run the current print shop amount to \$50,000 annually, and all current print shop personnel would be retained if the expansion takes place.

After discussing the print shop situation with Northwest Suburban's chief financial officer, Susan defined three possible print shop alternatives:

1. *Close the print shop completely.* Use outside vendors for all printing.
2. *Expand the print shop as envisioned.* Essentially, this option means expanding the print shop and performing all feasible work in-house. Under this proposal, the shop would remain under SUPPORT and thus would present no tax consequences.
3. *Expand the print shop as in Alternative 2, but transfer all printing activities to PROPERTIES.* In this situation, capital expenses, such as depreciation and lease payments, would be tax deductible; however, all profits would be taxable. The primary motivation behind this alternative is to permit the print shop to enter the for-profit commercial printing business.

Regarding Alternative 1, many outsiders to the hospital industry would be surprised at the amount of outsourcing that takes place. The business of running a hospital is extremely complicated, and many facets of a hospital's operations can be more efficiently run by outside companies that specialize in specific functions. The three most commonly outsourced functions (by number of hospitals) are laundry, housekeeping, and clinical/diagnostic equipment maintenance. However, this list goes on and on. In fact, a significant number of hospitals are now outsourcing some patient care (clinical) services, the most common being anesthesia, emergency department, dialysis, and imaging services. Some hospitals are outsourcing to such a degree that they have created the position of COO—not chief operating officer, but chief outsourcing officer.

Northwest Suburban's corporate cost of capital, which is dominated by hospital operations, is estimated to be 8.4 percent. However, the system also computes divisional costs of capital for each subsidiary. SUPPORT has access to municipal debt that currently costs about 5.5 percent. Its target capital structure consists of 60 percent debt and 40 percent equity (fund) financing. Because SUPPORT has a captive business relationship with Northwest Suburban's four hospitals, it has relatively low business risk and, consequently, a relatively low cost of equity of 13.0 percent.

PROPERTIES cannot issue municipal debt. The bulk of its debt consists of mortgage loans provided by banks and insurance companies. Mortgage debt, which is secured by pledged property, has a relatively low interest rate for taxable debt. Currently, this rate is 7.5 percent. The combined federal-plus-state tax rate of PROPERTIES is 30 percent. Because PROPERTIES competes with other property development companies, its inherent business risk is high, and hence it has a relatively high cost of equity of 17 percent. However, its ability to use real estate as collateral for its debt financing gives it a relatively high debt capacity—about 75 percent. Northwest Suburban's capital budgeting policy guidelines call for all cash-flow analyses to be restricted to a five-year horizon with zero end-of-project salvage values. The rationale is that estimating cash flows any further into the future is just too difficult.

It is now December 2021, and the print shop analysis is due in one week. Thus, for simplicity, assume that all capital investment cash flows and lease payments for 2022 occur at the beginning of 2022 (the end of 2021). Then, the five years of operating flows occur from 2022 through 2026. In addition, Northwest Suburban's capital budgeting policy is to assume that all costs and prices that are not fixed by contract will increase at a 3 percent inflation rate. Thus, any 2021 dollar costs must be increased by 3 percent annually beginning in 2022. Furthermore, any 2021 volume amounts must be increased by 2 percent annually, beginning in 2022.

In regard to the feasibility of entering the commercial printing business should the print shop be placed into PROPERTIES, Susan discussed the profitability of commercial printing businesses with Mark Stanton, president of the Land of Lincoln Printers Association, the state trade organization. Mark pointed out that the average printer in the United States has a profit margin of 5.5 percent, while the average in the Chicago metropolitan area is barely 4 percent. Return on assets in the industry is 7.5 percent nationwide and 5.2 percent locally.

Estimates regarding the profits that could be earned on commercial printing sales are far from precise, but the best guess is that in 2022 commercial sales could bring in as much as $80,000 in pretax profits (in 2022 dollars). This amount could increase to $100,000 in 2023 (in 2023 dollars), given more time to advertise and build customer relationships. Although very uncertain, the pretax profits that stem from external business are expected to increase by 5 percent per year after 2023, including both volume growth and price inflation. Note that the pretax profit amounts include all costs related to the external printing business except marketing costs, which are estimated to be $6,000 in 2022 and are expected to increase at the 3 percent inflation rate.

Finally, Northwest Suburban's purchasing manager has questioned the system's policy regarding external printing contracts: What is the current policy, and might a change in policy have a bearing on the decision at hand? The discount rate to use in the analysis has also been an issue under discussion. Susan believes that the discount rate should reflect the divisional placement of the print shop, but some staffers have disagreed with this view. "After all," said one, "the primary factor in choosing a discount rate is the riskiness of the cash flows being discounted."

You are the administrative resident at Northwest Suburban and have been given the task of analyzing the feasibility of the print shop and recommending a course of action. In assigning the project, your preceptor indicated that a risk analysis was appropriate. When asked for more guidance, his response was, "You know more about this sort of thing than I do. Just do it!"

EXHIBIT 23.1 Northwest Suburban Health System: Printing Currently Done by Outside Vendors

	Fiscal Year	
	2020	*2021*
Graphics Printing		
Mercury	$ 85,002.31	$ 7,727.86
Universal Color Graphics	16,982.44	12,588.00
Windy City Press	9,300.00	24,446.00
Northern Illinois Printing	5,628.50	711.94
Pickett Press	3,526.14	2,337.10
Sir Speedy	1,962.58	8,939.50
Northwest Suburban Printing	85.46	0.00
C & S Printing	1,161.00	0.00
Great Lakes Printing Service	0.00	75,292.83
Total graphics printing	$123,648.43	$132,043.23
90% to be brought in-house	$111,283.59	$118,838.91
Forms Printing		
Continuous	$223,826.43	$239,493.82
Stock tab	77,150.41	82,550.50
Labels	68,032.88	65,965.88
Carbon snap	97,563.27	106,283.44
Envelopes	61,096.52	62,435.89
Lab mount	5,095.35	5,126.33
Flat 1/2 side	42,266.69	40,986.45
Special	39,910.37	46,295.47
Oversize	1,458.19	0.00
Special service	1,190.00	2,743.98
Card stock	21,237.40	23,479.11
NCR flat	21,017.01	22,798.19
Total forms printing	$659,844.52	$698,159.06
50% to be brought in-house	$329,922.26	$349,079.53
Total vendor printing	$783,492.95	$830,202.29
Total to be brought in-house	$441,205.85	$467,918.44

EXHIBIT 23.2
Northwest Suburban Health System: Equipment Capital Investment Requirements

Item	*Estimated Cost*
Two-color press	$ 65,000
Two-color press (small), Model 9860	26,000
Ten-hole drill press	7,800
Futura F-20 folder system	13,000
Collator-stitcher, 12 bin	28,000
Bookmaker, Michael 1000E	5,300
Camera with processor	14,000
Paper plate, AB Dick 148	11,500
Three-knife trimmer	12,000
Infrared dryer systems (2)	5,000
Delivery van	25,000
Miscellaneous items	5,000
Total capital investment	$217,600

EXHIBIT 23.3
Northwest Suburban Health System: Print Shop's Incremental Labor Costs (in 2021 Dollars)

Number	*Position*	*Annual Salary*
1	Lead printer	$ 42,000
1	Delivery person	25,000
1	Clerical assistant	15,000
	Projected raw-labor expense	$ 82,000
	Plus: 20 percent fringe benefits	16,400
	Total annual incremental labor costs	$ 98,400

PART IX

FINANCIAL CONDITION ANALYSIS AND FORECASTING

CASE 24

COMMONWEALTH HEALTH PLANS

ASSESSING HMO PERFORMANCE

Commonwealth Health Plans is one of Virginia's largest managed care organizations (MCOs). In fact, it is the largest of the state's not-for-profit MCOs. It offers prepaid health coverage to more than 500,000 members in 17 counties, which include the following major cities: Richmond, Norfolk, Virginia Beach, Arlington, Alexandria, and Roanoke.

Commonwealth's various products include commercial health maintenance organizations (HMOs), Medicare HMOs (Medicare Advantage plans), preferred provider organizations (PPOs), and point-of-service (POS) plans. These plans are all designed to meet the needs of a wide segment of Virginia's population of approximately 8.5 million. The revenue breakdown of plan types is as follows:

Plan Type	*Percentage of Revenue*
Commercial HMO	46%
Medicare HMO	39
PPO	10
POS	5
	100%

Commonwealth was the first MCO in Virginia to seek and receive accreditation from the National Committee for Quality Assurance (NCQA), and each of its component plans has been rated as excellent, the highest accreditation level. The NCQA judges a health plan on its performance in three areas: clinical performance (based on HEDIS [Healthcare Effectiveness Data and Information Set] results), member satisfaction (based on CAHPS [Consumer Assessment of Healthcare Providers and Systems] results), and key structures and processes. HEDIS and CAHPS scores together account for about 40 percent of the assessment for HMOs, with performance against structure and process standards accounting for the remaining 60 percent. All three areas are important, and together they give an accurate overall assessment of the quality of a health plan. (For more information on the NCQA, visit its website at www.ncqa.org.)

A summary of Commonwealth's 2020 and 2021 HMO plan financial data (including both commercial and Medicare) is presented in exhibit 24.1, and exhibit 24.2 contains a summary of operating and enrollment data. To help in analyzing Commonwealth's performance, its managers have classified the following four Virginia HMOs as primary competitors.

HMO	*Number of Counties Served*	*2021 Total Enrollment*	*2021 Total Assets (in Thousands)*
WellLife	23	516,858	$408,707
Signet Healthcare	15	360,252	178,662
Proxima	15	247,109	144,982
Sparta	28	205,296	103,504

These plans have the geographic coverage and financial resources to be prominent players in the Virginia managed care industry. Furthermore, the primary competitors are operating in the same service areas and have a similar product mix as Commonwealth and hence are potential threats to its future success. In addition to comparisons with national data, all internal analyses that use benchmarking compare Commonwealth's performance with the state average and the primary competitor list. **Note, however, that not all relevant performance measures have a complete set of comparative data available.**

Exhibit 24.3 contains selected financial and operating ratios for Commonwealth's primary competitors as well as the means and medians for all Virginia HMOs. Exhibit 24.4 contains selected national data, in which all comparative data are for HMO plans only. Exhibit 24.5 contains selected ratio definitions.

You have just started an administrative residency at Commonwealth. On your first day at the organization, CEO Roberta Osborne stated that the best way to get to know the financial and operating condition of any business is to complete a brief financial statement and operating indicator analysis, and assigned you to do so. Although you agree that this is a great way to learn more about Commonwealth and its competitors' HMO plans, you wonder whether she has any hidden motives. Perhaps Commonwealth is having financial problems with these plans and Roberta thinks that you can spot them, or perhaps she just wants to test your analytical skills.

In any event, she has already scheduled a financial and operating performance analyses presentation for the next executive committee meeting as a way for you to demonstrate your skills to Commonwealth's senior managers. In preparing for the meeting, you called Amity Wallace, the previous administrative resident, to get some advice for your presentation to the executive committee. Amity just left Commonwealth for a job with Humana. Her advice was to do a standard financial statement analysis, including statement of cash flow analysis, DuPont analysis, and ratio and operating indicator analyses.

Your first impression was that this task should be a "piece of cake," as you had performed a similar analysis for a hospital during your internship. However, as you began the task, it became apparent that the ratios used and their interpretations differ across industries; that is, the ratios that are critical to identifying the financial condition of a hospital are not necessarily the same ratios that are critical to a managed care plan. In addition, many of the ratios that are relevant to both hospitals and managed care plans have values that differ substantially.

Consider the medical loss ratio (defined as medical expenses divided by premium revenue), which measures the proportion of premium revenue that is spent on providing member healthcare services. Clearly, this ratio is not applicable to providers such as hospitals. The Affordable Care Act requires that large group insurance plans spend at least 85 percent of premiums on medical services. If they fail to do so, then insurers should pay a rebate to customers. (Does Commonwealth meet this requirement? Also, what do you think of the choice of terminology for the medical loss ratio?)

To help the executive committee interpret your presentation, you plan to point out key differences between your analysis for a health plan and an analysis for a hospital as they emerge. In addition, you know that identifying key areas of concern and recommending courses of action is more important than merely going over the numbers.

EXHIBIT 24.1
Commonwealth Health Plans: HMO Plan Financial Data (in Millions of Dollars)

	2020	2021
Statements of Operations		
Premium revenue	$313.7	$357.6
Interest income	2.4	3.5
Total revenues	$316.1	$361.1
Operating expenses		
Medical costs	$263.0	$291.8
Selling and administrative	36.8	43.6
Depreciation	4.7	5.0
Total operating expenses	$304.5	$340.4
Net income	$ 11.6	$ 20.7
Balance Sheets		
Cash	$ 37.2	$ 27.2
Marketable securities	42.7	60.9
Premiums receivable	3.7	7.4
Total current assets	$ 83.6	$ 95.5
Net fixed assets	30.0	31.7
Total assets	$113.6	$127.2
Medical costs payable	$ 44.8	$ 48.7
Accounts payable/accruals	15.4	17.3
Total current liabilities	$ 60.2	$ 66.0
Long-term debt	17.1	4.2
Net assets (equity)	36.3	57.0
Total liabilities and net assets	$113.6	$127.2
Other Data		
Medical loss ratio	83.8%	81.6%
Administrative cost ratio	13.2%	13.6%
Total commercial premium revenue	$170.9	$205.6
Total Medicare revenue	$142.8	$152.0
Total physician services expense	$125.6	$127.1
Total inpatient expense	$ 80.8	$ 90.1
Total other medical expense	$ 56.6	$ 74.6

EXHIBIT 24.2
Commonwealth Health Plans: HMO Plan Operating and Enrollment Data (in Millions of Dollars)

	2020	2021
Commercial premium revenue PMPM	$ 127.82	$ 127.90
Medicare revenue PMPM	$ 449.37	$ 437.23
Commercial patient days per 1,000 enrollees	302.9	266.4
Medicare patient days per 1,000 enrollees	1,622.4	1,418.1
Commercial member-months	1,337,036	1,607,036
Commercial physician encounters	594,381	622,749
Commercial inpatient days	43,661	39,763
Medicare member-months	317,778	347,643
Medicare physician encounters	149,622	185,283

PMPM: per member per month

EXHIBIT 24.3
Selected State HMO Industry Financial and Operating Data (in Millions of Dollars)

	2020	2021
Total Margin		
WellLife	4.8%	5.8%
Signet Healthcare	3.0	3.2
Proxima	9.1	(0.7)
Sparta	10.5	9.1
State average	3.8	(3.9)
State median	4.8	4.7
Percent Administrative Expense		
WellLife	12.1%	11.5%
Signet Healthcare	12.2	13.4
Proxima	13.6	16.4
Sparta	23.9	26.8
State average	15.5	17.4
State median	14.8	15.7
Percent Inpatient Expense		
WellLife	32.2%	30.3%
Signet Healthcare	22.8	22.4
Proxima	21.2	23.0
Sparta	18.2	18.8
State average	25.2	23.3
State median	23.6	24.3

(continued)

EXHIBIT 24.3 Selected State HMO Industry Financial and Operating Data (in Millions of Dollars) (continued)

	2020	2021
Percent Physician Expense		
WellLife	54.1%	56.9%
Signet Healthcare	31.3	30.3
Proxima	22.7	24.9
Sparta	12.8	18.6
State average	28.8	31.3
State median	31.1	31.6
Percent Other Medical Expense		
WellLife	0.1%	0.1%
Signet Healthcare	8.9	7.8
Proxima	27.5	30.2
Sparta	45.7	35.0
State average	14.6	12.5
State median	10.2	8.9
Commercial Premium Revenue PMPM		
WellLife	$108.68	$110.19
Signet Healthcare	39.86	27.50
Proxima	120.68	124.27
Sparta	88.41	95.06
State average	101.17	102.53
State median	108.32	108.95
Medicare Revenue PMPM		
WellLife	$406.57	$421.57
Signet Healthcare	N/A	N/A
Proxima	N/A	N/A
Sparta	N/A	N/A
State average	365.12	376.04
State median	426.18	430.57
Commercial Inpatient Days per 1,000 Enrollees		
WellLife	245.4	246.0
Signet Healthcare	258.4	248.8
Proxima	251.8	259.2
Sparta	198.2	248.9
State average	278.0	237.0
State median	279.1	248.8

EXHIBIT 24.3 Selected State HMO Industry Financial and Operating Data (in Millions of Dollars) (continued)

	2020	*2021*
Medicare Inpatient Days per 1,000 Enrollees		
WellLife	1,388.4	1,323.8
Signet Healthcare	1,165.2	1,188.7
Proxima	1,518.8	1,382.2
Sparta	1,623.8	1,566.9
State average	1,432.1	1,375.5
State median	1,380.5	1,350.6
Commercial Physician Encounters per Member		
WellLife	2.2	3.6
Signet Healthcare	1.5	1.4
Proxima	2.7	2.6
Sparta	3.5	3.6
State average	3.8	3.8
State median	3.9	3.7
Medicare Physician Encounters per Member		
WellLife	9.8	9.6
Signet Healthcare	6.6	6.9
Proxima	10.1	10.0
Sparta	11.2	11.3
State average	9.1	9.1
State median	8.6	8.9

N/A: not available or applicable; PMPM: per member per month

Note: The Virginia data for the HMO industry contained in this exhibit are for illustrative purposes only. These data should not be used to conduct actual financial analyses.

EXHIBIT 24.4
Selected 2021 National HMO Industry Financial and Operating Data

Average copay per office visit	$ 8
Average copay per hospitalization	$36
Average copay per pharmacy prescription	$ 7
Medical Loss Ratio	
Upper quartile	89.0%
Median	84.9
Lower quartile	80.0
Administrative Cost Ratio	
Upper quartile	14.4%
Median	12.0
Lower quartile	9.0
Operating Margin	
Upper quartile	5.0%
Median	2.5
Lower quartile	1.1
Total Margin	
Upper quartile	5.5%
Median	2.9
Lower quartile	1.5
Return on Assets (ROA)	
Upper quartile	16.5%
Median	11.3
Lower quartile	4.8
Return on Equity (ROE)	
Upper quartile	50.2%
Median	31.4
Lower quartile	18.2
Current Ratio	
Upper quartile	1.29
Median	0.95
Lower quartile	0.49
Days Cash on Hand	
Upper quartile	32.7
Median	10.3
Lower quartile	0.8

EXHIBIT 24.4
Selected 2021 National HMO Industry Financial and Operating Data (continued)

Current Asset Turnover	
Upper quartile	14.1
Median	6.4
Lower quartile	3.7
Total Asset Turnover	
Upper quartile	4.1
Median	3.1
Lower quartile	2.2
Days Premiums Receivable	
Upper quartile	14.0
Median	8.9
Lower quartile	7.0
Debt Ratio	
Upper quartile	81.3%
Median	68.4
Lower quartile	59.7

Note: The national data for the HMO industry contained in this exhibit are for illustrative purposes only. These data should not be used to conduct actual financial analyses.

EXHIBIT 24.5 Selected Ratio Definitions

Medical Loss Ratio	$\frac{\text{Medical expenses}}{\text{Premium revenue}}$
Administrative Cost Ratio	$\frac{\text{Selling and administrative expenses + Depreciation}}{\text{Premium revenue}}$
Operating Margin	$\frac{\text{Net income – Interest income}}{\text{Premium revenue}}$
Percent Administrative Expense	$\frac{\text{Selling and administrative expense}}{\text{Total operating expenses}}$
Percent Inpatient Expense	$\frac{\text{Inpatient expense}}{\text{Total operating expenses}}$
Percent Physician Expense	$\frac{\text{Physician services expense}}{\text{Total operating expenses}}$
Percent Other Medical Expense	$\frac{\text{Other medical expense}}{\text{Total operating expenses}}$

CASE 25

RIVER COMMUNITY HOSPITAL (A)

ASSESSING HOSPITAL PERFORMANCE

River Community Hospital is a 210-bed, not-for-profit, acute care hospital with a long-standing reputation for providing quality healthcare services to a growing service area. River competes with three other hospitals in its metropolitan statistical area—two not-for-profits and one for-profit. It is the smallest of the four but has traditionally been ranked highest in patient satisfaction polls.

Hospitals are accredited by The Joint Commission, an independent, not-for-profit organization whose mission is to improve the safety and quality of healthcare provided to the public through accreditation and related services. (For more information on The Joint Commission, visit its website at www.jointcommission.org.) Although accreditation is optional for hospitals, it is generally required to qualify for governmental (Medicare and Medicaid) reimbursement, and hence most hospitals apply for accreditation. River passed its latest Joint Commission survey, receiving its Gold Seal of Approval.

In recent years, competition among the four hospitals in River's service area has been keen but friendly. However, a large for-profit chain recently purchased the for-profit hospital, resulting in some anxiety among the managers of the other three hospitals because of the chain's reputation for aggressively increasing market share in the markets they serve.

Relevant financial and operating data for River are contained in exhibits 25.1 through 25.5, and selected peer group data are contained in the case spreadsheet. In addition to the data in the exhibits, the following information was extracted from the notes section of River's 2021 annual report.

1. *A significant portion of River's net patient service revenue was generated by patients who are covered either by Medicare, Medicaid, or other government programs or by various private plans, including managed care plans, that have contracts with River and specify discounts from charges.* In general, the proportional amount of deductions is similar between inpatients and outpatients. A breakdown of the gross and net patient service revenues and operating expenses for both inpatient and outpatient services is given in exhibit 25.5.
2. *River has a contributory money accumulation (defined contribution) pension plan that covers most of its employees.* Participants can contribute up to 20 percent of earnings to the pension plan. River matches, on a dollar-for-dollar basis, employee contributions of up to 2 percent of wages and pays 50 cents on the dollar for contributions of more than 2 percent and up to 4 percent. Because the plan is a defined contribution plan (as opposed to a defined benefit plan), River has no unfunded pension liabilities. Pension expense was approximately \$0.543 million in 2020 and \$0.588 million in 2021.
3. *River is a member of the State Hospital Trust Fund, under which it purchases professional liability insurance coverage for individual claims up to \$1 million (subject to a deductible of \$100,000 per claim).* River is self-insured for amounts of more than \$1 million but less than \$5 million. Any liability award in excess of \$5 million is covered by a commercial liability policy. For example, the policy pays \$2 million on a \$7 million award. River is currently involved in eight suits involving claims of various amounts that could ultimately be tried before a jury. Determining the exact potential liability in these claims is impossible, but management does not believe that the settlement of these cases would have a material effect on River's financial position.

You have just joined the River staff as a special assistant to the CEO. On your first day on the job, the CEO, Melissa Randolph, stated that the best way to get to know the financial and operating conditions of the hospital is to conduct thorough financial statement and operating indicator analyses, and so she assigned you this task. Although you agree that such analyses are a good way to get started, you wonder whether Melissa has any ulterior motives. Perhaps the hospital is having problems and she thinks that you can spot them, or perhaps she wants to test your analytical skills. Melissa is from the "old school" of hospital management and has been looking for someone to bring modern management methods to the hospital.

As you prepare for the analyses, several relevant factors come to light. First, in reviewing the policy decisions made by River's board of trustees over the past decade, you note that in 2020 the board made the decision to significantly expand River's outpatient services. The rationale was that many procedures historically done on an inpatient basis were now being done in an outpatient setting, and if River did not offer such services it would lose the patients to other providers.

Second, the board chair has great concerns about the decline in profitability between 2020 and 2021. Perhaps because she is CEO of a local company, the chair focuses on return on equity (ROE) as the key measure of profitability. She has requested that management develop some strategies to improve profitability and estimate the impact of the strategies on River's ROE.

Third, the hospital had difficulties making payments on its long-term debt several years ago. As a consequence, the hospital's long-term debt agreement now includes a covenant that requires the hospital to maintain a current ratio of at least 3.75. Debt covenants are limits or thresholds for certain financial ratios that the company may not breach. Violating a covenant means that a lender can legally call the debt, or demand repayment in full, and the board of River Community Hospital strongly wants to avoid this situation.

Finally, board members were complaining that too much time is being spent at quarterly board meetings discussing River's financial condition. "There is so much to accomplish that we just don't have the time to consider a large number of ratios at each meeting," said one member.

You know that many healthcare providers are now using dashboards to focus on key performance indicators (KPIs). A dashboard is nothing more than a way to summarize an organization's financial and operating performance. Of course, the name stems from an automobile's dashboard, which contains gauges that give drivers essential information about the car's performance and operating condition. Thus, you plan to develop two dashboards, each containing no more than five KPIs. One dashboard will use financial ratios to focus on financial performance, while the other will use operating indicator ratios to focus on operating performance. At the next board meeting, you plan to present your recommendations for the contents of these dashboards along with the rationale for the ratios chosen. Your ultimate goal is to replace the full financial and operating performance discussion at future board meetings with a limited discussion of the KPIs.

EXHIBIT 25.1 River Community Hospital: Statements of Operations and Changes in Net Assets (in Thousands of Dollars)

	2021	*2020*	*2019*
Revenues			
Net patient service revenue	$148,118	$121,765	$119,845
Premium revenue	17,316	16,455	15,543
Other revenue	3,079	2,704	2,397
Net operating revenue	$168,513	$140,924	$137,785
Expenses			
Salaries and benefits	$126,223	$102,334	$101,996
Supplies	20,568	18,673	17,854
Insurance	4,518	3,710	3,678
Purchased services	3,189	2,603	2,543
Depreciation	3,965	2,198	2,091
Interest	5,329	3,476	3,122
Total expenses	$163,792	$132,994	$131,284
Operating Income	$ 4,721	$ 7,930	$ 6,501
Nonoperating Income			
Contributions	$ 243	$ 198	$ 151
Investment income	3,870	3,678	3,497
Total nonoperating income	$ 4,113	$ 3,876	$ 3,648
Excess of revenues over expenses (net income)	$ 8,834	$ 11,806	$ 10,149

EXHIBIT 25.1
River Community Hospital: Statements of Operations and Changes in Net Assets (in Thousands of Dollars) (continued)

	2021	2020	2019
Changes in Net Assets			
Without donor restrictions:			
Excess of revenues over expenses	$ 8,834	$11,806	$10,149
Increase in net assets without donor restrictions	$ 8,834	$11,806	$10,149
With donor restrictions:			
Gifts and bequests	$ 1,466	$ 900	$ 466
Increase in net assets with donor restrictions	$ 1,466	$ 900	$ 466
Increase in net assets	$10,300	$12,706	$10,615
Net assets at beginning of year	$54,174	$41,468	$30,853
Net assets at end of year	$64,474	$54,174	$41,468

EXHIBIT 25.2
River Community Hospital: Balance Sheets (in Thousands of Dollars)

	2021	2020	2019
Assets			
Current assets			
Cash and cash equivalents	$ 16,468	$ 10,852	$ 8,765
Short-term investments	10,000	5,000	5,000
Net patient accounts receivable	28,509	25,927	24,504
Inventories	3,695	2,302	1,629
Total current assets	$ 58,672	$ 44,081	$ 39,898
Long-term investments	$ 18,059	$ 25,837	$ 17,170
Net property and equipment	88,490	53,149	53,394
Total assets	$165,221	$123,067	$110,462
Liabilities and Equity			
Current liabilities			
Notes payable	$ 4,334	$ 3,345	$ 3,345
Accounts payable	5,022	6,933	7,899
Accrued expenses	6,069	5,037	4,172
Total current liabilities	$ 15,425	$ 15,315	$ 15,416
Long-term debt	85,322	53,578	53,578
Total liabilities	$100,747	$ 68,893	$ 68,994
Net assets (equity)			
Without donor restrictions	$ 56,168	$ 46,434	$ 34,162
With donor restrictions	8,306	7,740	7,306
Total net assets	$ 64,474	$ 54,174	$ 41,468
Total liabilities and net assets	$165,221	$123,067	$110,462

Net Property and Equipment (thousands of dollars)

	2021	2020	2019
Land	$ 2,954	$ 2,035	$ 2,000
Buildings and equipment	115,595	77,208	75,290
Gross property and equipment	$118,549	$ 79,243	$ 77,290
Less: Accumulated depreciation	30,059	26,094	23,896
Net property and equipment	$ 88,490	$ 53,149	$ 53,394

EXHIBIT 25.3
River Community Hospital: Statements of Cash Flows (in Thousands of Dollars)

	2021	*2020*
Cash Flows from Operating Activities		
Operating income	$ 4,721	$ 7,930
Adjustments		
Depreciation	$ 3,965	$ 2,198
Increase in net patient accounts receivable	(2,582)	(1,423)
Increase in inventories	(1,393)	(673)
Decrease in accounts payable	(1,911)	(966)
Increase in accrued expenses	1,032	865
Net cash from operations	$ 3,832	$ 7,931
Cash Flows from Investing Activities		
Capital expenditures	($39,306)	($ 1,953)
Nonoperating income	4,113	3,876
Purchase of short-term securities	(5,000)	0
Purchase/sale of long-term securities	7,778	(8,667)
Net cash from investing	($32,415)	($ 6,744)
Cash Flows from Financing Activities		
Restricted gifts and bequests	$ 1,466	$ 900
Proceeds from bank loan (notes payable)	989	0
Proceeds from issuance of long-term debt	31,744	0
Net cash from financing	$34,199	$ 900
Net increase (decrease) in cash	$ 5,616	$ 2,087
Cash and cash equivalents, beginning of year	$10,852	$ 8,765
Cash and cash equivalents, end of year	$16,468	$10,852

EXHIBIT 25.4 River Community Hospital: Selected Operating Data

	2021	2020	2019
Medicare discharges	2,741	2,860	2,721
Total discharges	5,489	5,324	5,622
Outpatient visits	97,141	86,798	85,232
Licensed beds	210	210	210
Staffed beds	178	197	193
Patient days	32,050	33,947	35,268
All-payer case mix index	1.3161	1.2993	1.2869
Full-time equivalents	619.3	625.8	610.8

EXHIBIT 25.5 River Community Hospital: Operating Revenue and Expense Allocation (in Thousands of Dollars)

	2021	2020	2019
Operating Revenue			
Gross inpatient service	$161,265	$155,243	$153,594
Gross outpatient service	$221,718	$151,113	$133,459
Gross patient service revenue	$382,983	$306,356	$287,053
Contractual allowances	$214,470	$165,432	$149,268
Net operating revenue	$168,513	$140,924	$137,785
Operating Expenses			
Inpatient service	$ 72,996	$ 70,218	$ 71,852
Outpatient service	$ 90,796	$ 62,776	$ 59,432
Total operating expenses	$163,792	$132,994	$131,284

CASE

26

RIVER COMMUNITY HOSPITAL (B)

FINANCIAL FORECASTING

River Community Hospital is a 210-bed, not-for-profit, acute care hospital with a long-standing reputation for providing quality healthcare services to a growing service area. River competes with three other hospitals in its metropolitan statistical area—two not-for-profits and one for-profit. It is the smallest of the four but has traditionally been ranked highest in patient satisfaction polls. For a complete description of the hospital, along with its 2019–2021 financial statements, see case 25 (River Community Hospital [A]).

As the newly hired special assistant to the CEO, you have completed the financial and operating analyses (see case 25) assigned by your boss, Melissa Randolph. In fact, your presentation on these analyses to the board of trustees went so well that Melissa asked you to present River's preliminary five-year financial plan at the next board meeting. She provided the following guidelines to aid in the planning process:

1. *Use your own best judgment to create River's financial plan, relying on your knowledge of the historical situation of the hospital, current trends in the healthcare industry, and the competitive environment facing hospitals today.* Make any assumptions you believe to be necessary to create the plan, including assumptions about inpatient and outpatient volume growth, capacity constraints, reimbursement patterns, hospital staffing patterns, and input cost inflation. Completely document your assumptions in your report. **You have limited specific information about River, so use your**

general knowledge about trends in the hospital industry to make the forecasts. The quality of your financial plan will be judged as much (or more) on the validity of your assumptions as on the mechanics of the forecasting process.

2. *Place emphasis on the forecast for the first year (2022).* In addition, create rough income statements, balance sheets, and statements of cash flows for the following four years (five years in total), including key financial ratios.
3. *Keep in mind the five primary methods for forecasting income statement items and balance sheet accounts.* These methods are (a) percentage of sales (in which a constant growth rate is applied), (b) simple linear regression, (c) curvilinear regression, (d) multiple regression, and (e) specific item forecasting. You may need to use several of these methods in your forecasts. (Hint: Do not forget that spreadsheets have a regression capability.)
4. *Use the financial analysis data from case 25 (if that case is assigned) to help with your forecasts.* Those areas where hospital performance has been poor should be improved, and your forecasts should reflect anticipated operational improvements where applicable.
5. *Do not get so involved in the mechanics of the forecasting process that you forget to apply common sense to your forecasts.* Think about what has happened in the past and what is likely to happen in the future regarding utilization, prices, costs, and asset requirements. If a forecast does not make sense, modify it until it does. For example, a blind application of statistical forecasting techniques might lead to a forecast containing five years of net operating losses. Regardless of statistical "fit," such a forecast makes no sense because any hospital that expects to survive will have to take actions to change utilization, pricing, or cost trends to ensure positive operating results. Thus, the "blindly" forecasted values do not represent what is likely to happen in the future, even though they might be a perfect reflection of historical trends. Similarly, a forecast that is wildly optimistic probably needs to be modified because payers and competitors likely would react to dampen profitability if it rose dramatically.

In closing, Melissa gave you her view of a good financial plan: "First and foremost, the plan should consist of pro forma financial statements along with a table that summarizes the amount of financing generated internally and any external financing requirements. Second, key financial ratios should be calculated, and the hospital's expected future financial condition should be assessed, with special emphasis on changes from the hospital's current condition. Third, make sure that your forecasted financial statements are consistent with one another. The last special assistant could not figure out that two balance sheet accounts—equity (fund) capital and accumulated depreciation—are tied to income statement items, so he did not last very long. Finally, make all your assumptions clear, and be prepared to answer questions from the board concerning the impact of changes in your assumptions on the financial plan."

PART

CURRENT ASSET MANAGEMENT

X

CASE 27

MOUNTAIN VILLAGE CLINIC

CASH BUDGETING

Mountain Village Clinic is a small walk-in clinic adjacent to the primary ski area of Mountain Village, a winter resort located a short distance from Aspen, Colorado. It should be no surprise that the clinic specializes in the treatment of injuries sustained while skiing. It is owned and operated by two physicians: James Peterson, an orthopedist, and Amanda Cook, an internist. Patient volume at Mountain Village is highly seasonal because most of the business occurs during the ski season, which generally runs from December through March. In fact, at one time Drs. Peterson and Cook thought about closing Mountain Village during the slow months, but (1) the clinic would be difficult to operate efficiently for only a portion of the year and (2) the area has started to attract a sizable number of summer visitors, which has made summer operations more financially attractive.

Mountain Village has an outside accountant who takes care of payroll matters, but Dr. Cook does all the other financial work for the clinic. However, to help in that task, Mountain Village recently hired a part-time MHA student, Doug Washington. On a Wednesday afternoon in October 2021, Dr. Cook called Doug into her office to tell him about an upcoming meeting with the head of commercial lending at First Bank of Aspen, Mountain Village's primary lender. The purpose of the meeting is to discuss cash management services and the clinic's line-of-credit requirements. A line of credit is a short-term loan agreement by which a bank agrees to lend a business some specified maximum amount. The business can borrow (draw down) against the credit line at any time it is in force, which typically is no longer than one year. When a line expires, it must be renegotiated if it is still needed. The amount borrowed on the line, or some lesser amount, can be repaid at any time, but any amount outstanding must be repaid at expiration. Interest is charged on the amount drawn down, and a commitment fee is often required up front to secure the line. In general, lines of credit are used by businesses to meet temporary (usually seasonal) cash needs as opposed to permanent long-term financing purposes. Currently, the annual interest rate on a First Bank line of credit is 4 percent (compounded monthly), and First Bank pays a 2 percent annual interest rate (compounded monthly) on temporary deposits of excess cash in a savings account. Interest earned (paid) occurs in the month following the end-of-month cash surplus (loan requirement).

To prepare for the upcoming meeting with the bank, Dr. Cook asked Doug to develop a cash budget and determine the line-of-credit amount that Mountain Village should request. No one had taken the time to prepare a cash budget recently, although a spreadsheet model that had been constructed a few years ago was available for use. From information previously developed, Doug knew that no seasonal financing would be needed from First Bank before January, so he decided to restrict his budget to the period of January through June 2022.

As a first step, Doug looked through Mountain Village's financial records to get the data needed to develop the billings forecast, which is contained in exhibit 27.1. He assumed that actual billings as a percentage of forecast would be 100 percent. On the basis of Mountain Village's previous collections experience, he was able to convert billings for medical services into actual cash collections. On average, about 25 percent of the billings are collected in the month of billing (1–30 days), 30 percent in the first month after billing (31–60 days), and 40 percent in the second month after billing (61–90 days); 5 percent of the billings are never collected (bad debt).

Variable medical costs at Mountain Village are assumed to consist entirely of medical and administrative supplies. These supplies, which are estimated to cost 15 percent of billings, are purchased two months before expected usage. On average, the clinic pays about half of its suppliers in the month of purchase (two months before use) and the other half in the following month (one month before use).

Clinical labor costs (for physicians and other clinical employees) are the primary expense of Mountain Village. During the high season (December through March), these costs run $300,000 a month, but some of the clinical staff work only seasonally, so clinical labor costs drop to $240,000 a month in the remaining months.

Mountain Village pays fixed general and administrative expenses, including clerical labor, of approximately $60,000 per month, and a lease payment amounts to $24,000 per month. These expenditures are expected to continue at the same level throughout the forecast period. The clinic's monthly miscellaneous expenses are estimated to be $20,000.

Mountain Village has a semiannual, five-year, 5 percent, $500,000 term loan outstanding with First Bank for which payments are due on March 15 and September 15. Also, the clinic is planning to replace an old X-ray machine (which has no salvage value) in February with a new one that costs $250,000. Mountain Village is a partnership, so, for tax purposes, any profits (or losses) are prorated to the two physician partners, who must pay individual taxes on this income. Thus, no tax payments are built into the clinic's cash budget.

Mountain Village has to maintain a target cash balance of $50,000 at First Bank because of compensating balance requirements on its term loan. This amount of cash, but no more, is expected to be on hand on January 1, 2022.

For the daily cash budget, Doug made the following additional assumptions about volume and collections:

- Mountain Village operates seven days a week.
- Patient volume is more or less constant throughout the month, so the daily billings forecast will be 1/(number of days in the month) multiplied by the billings forecast for that month.
- Daily billings follow the 25 percent–30 percent–40 percent collection breakdown based on monthly billings.
- Collections are assumed to occur on the first day of the 1–30 days collections category (the day of billing), the first day of the 31–60 days collections category (31 days after the day of billing), and the first day of the 61–90 days collections category (61 days after the day of billing).
- Lease payment is made on the 1st of the month.
- Fifty percent of both clinical labor costs and general and administrative expenses are paid on the 1st of the month, and 50 percent are paid on the 15th of the month.
- Supplies are delivered on the 1st of the month and paid for on the 5th of the month.
- Miscellaneous expenses are incurred and paid evenly throughout each month.

- Term loan payments are made on the 15th of the month in which they are due.
- A target cash balance of $50,000 must be in the bank on each day.

Dr. Cook is highly risk averse and worries about the accuracy of Doug's cash budget, particularly if the actual billings and timing of billings collections and bad debt are different from the forecast. In addition, she was recently informed by First Bank that it is reviewing the amount of compensating balance requirements on Mountain Village's term loan, which would, in turn, affect the target cash balance it maintains. Finally, the cash at the beginning is a rough estimate and could be higher or lower than forecast.

Place yourself in Doug's position. Be prepared to discuss your analysis with Dr. Cook when you meet with her next week.

EXHIBIT 27.1
Mountain Village Clinic: Billings Forecast

Year	*Month*	*Amount*
2021	November	$300,000
	December	500,000
2022	January	700,000
	February	900,000
	March	600,000
	April	300,000
	May	200,000
	June	400,000
	July	500,000
	August	400,000

CASE 28

FOSTER PHARMACEUTICALS

RECEIVABLES MANAGEMENT

KATHLEEN GROGAN RECEIVED her PhD in pharmacology 10 years ago from Boston University. While there, she became interested in the business side of drug distribution and hence stayed on for an extra 18 months to earn an MBA. After graduation, she went to work for Capo Corporation, a major drug manufacturer, where she managed the development of a new nonprescription anti-allergy drug. Although the drug passed all US Food and Drug Administration (FDA) trials and was certified for general use, Capo simultaneously developed a similar drug that was cheaper to produce and equally effective in treating most, but not all, allergy symptoms. Thus, Capo decided not to proceed with production of the drug that Kathleen helped develop. However, Capo was willing to license production and distribution rights to another company. Kathleen thought that this might be a golden opportunity, so she quit her job with Capo to found her own company, Foster Pharmaceuticals. The sole purpose of Foster Pharmaceuticals is to obtain the license for, produce, and distribute the new drug, which Kathleen dubbed "SneezeRelief."

Kathleen is currently working on the business plan for Foster Pharmaceuticals, which she will present at a venture capital conference in New York. The main purpose of the conference is to match entrepreneurs with venture capitalists who are interested in providing capital to fledgling firms. She has spent a lot of time thinking about how Foster Pharmaceuticals' receivables should be managed. She is concerned about this issue because she knows of several small drug manufacturers that have gotten into serious financial difficulty because of poor receivables management.

Initially, Foster Pharmaceuticals would sell directly and exclusively to four retail customers in the northeast (exhibit 28.1 provides the sales mix). If demand proved solid, the company would expand into other areas and wholesale channels. Sales are expected to be highly seasonal: Allergy drug sales are slow during the winter months, but they pick up dramatically in the spring when plant pollen levels reach a peak. Business falls off again in the summer, but it picks up in the fall when the ragweed season begins. Kathleen's sales forecasts for the first six months of operations are given in exhibit 28.2. Assuming Foster Pharmaceuticals receives financing and begins operations, the sales forecasts for the first six months of the second year are provided in exhibit 28.3.

Kathleen does not plan to give discounts for early payment; discounts are not widely used in the industry. On the basis of preliminary discussions with retail outlets (Foster Pharmaceuticals customers), she forecasts the payment schedule shown in exhibit 28.4. She does not foresee any problems with bad-debt losses. First, the retailers with whom she plans to do business have been in operation for a long time. Second, she plans to carefully screen all customers. She believes these two factors will eliminate bad-debt losses. On average, she believes that 20 percent of receivables will contribute to profits, so 80 percent of receivables represent cash costs. Furthermore, the First National Bank of New England has indicated that its receivables financing would cost 8 percent annually.

Despite her optimism regarding bad-debt losses, Kathleen is concerned about Foster Pharmaceuticals' potential level of receivables, and she wants to put in place a monitoring system that will allow her to quickly spot any adverse trends that develop. The total sales forecast for the first full year of operations is 800,000 packages. Each package, which will contain 12 tablets, will be priced at $5.

Kathleen has hired you as an outside consultant to advise her about receivables management. So far, you have developed a model that produces accounts receivable balances, average collection period (ACP), aging schedules, uncollected balances schedules, and quarterly carrying costs for the end of March and the end of June. The uncollected balances schedule permits managers to remove the effects of seasonal and/or cyclical sales variation and to construct an accurate measure of receivables payment patterns. Thus, it provides financial managers with better aggregate information than do such crude measures as the ACP or aging schedule.

Kathleen anticipates that the venture capitalists at the conference will ask some questions concerning the interpretation of the receivables data, the sensitivity of the results to the basic assumptions, and the strategies to reduce carrying costs of receivables.

EXHIBIT 28.1
Foster Pharmaceuticals: Forecast Customer Sales Mix

Customer	*Sales Mix*
Large retail chain 1	40%
Large retail chain 2	35
Regional drug store	15
Small grocery chain	10

EXHIBIT 28.2
Foster Pharmaceuticals: Partial Sales Forecasts for Year 1

Month	*Sales*
January	$100,000
February	250,000
March	400,000
April	600,000
May	450,000
June	300,000

EXHIBIT 28.3
Foster Pharmaceuticals: Partial Sales Forecasts for Year 2

Month	*Sales*
January	$200,000
February	350,000
March	500,000
April	700,000
May	550,000
June	350,000

EXHIBIT 28.4
Foster Pharmaceuticals: Forecast Receivables Collection Pattern

Customer	*0–30 Days*	*31–60 Days*	*61–90 Days*
Large retail chain 1	35%	50%	15%
Large retail chain 2	25	40	35
Regional drug store	20	35	45
Small grocery chain	30	55	15

CASE 29

CLARINDA COMMUNITY HOSPITAL

INVENTORY MANAGEMENT

Clarinda Community Hospital is a 230-bed, not-for-profit, acute care hospital located in Clarinda, Iowa. The city is a typical Midwestern county seat and farming community best known as the birthplace of Glenn Miller, the famous big band leader of the late 1930s and early 1940s.

Clarinda carries more than 10,000 different items of inventory that vary widely in price, order lead times, and stockout costs. (Stockout costs are the total costs that result from running out of stock of a particular inventory item, including higher costs of service caused by scheduling delays or emergency replenishments as well as the costs associated with negative patient outcomes and potential lawsuits.) It uses the activity-based costing (ABC) method of inventory classification, also called "selective inventory control," along with a variety of inventory-control methods to manage its different inventory items.

The ABC classification system works this way: Clarinda maintains data on the average annual usage and unit cost of each inventory item, which is typically called a stock-keeping unit (SKU). Then, the dollar usage (average annual usage × unit cost) is calculated for each SKU. Next, these amounts are converted into percentages of total dollar usage, and the SKUs are arrayed from highest to lowest percentage. The SKUs are then divided into three groups (or classes)—labeled A, B, and C—using the general guidelines provided in exhibit 29.1.

To better use the limited resources available for inventory management, Clarinda's managers focus most of their attention on Class A items. The usage rates, stock positions, and delivery times for SKUs in this class are reviewed every other week, with control and ordering system data adjusted as necessary. Class B items are reviewed every quarter, while Class C items are reviewed semiannually.

Even though this process has served Clarinda well, Marco Muñoz, its new chief financial officer, thinks the hospital is carrying excess inventories. He notes that Clarinda has never come close to having a stockout, even when it has been running near 100 percent occupancy. He believes that a thorough review should be undertaken of all Class A items and that inventory turnover might be increased by 25 percent, and hence might lower inventory carrying costs, by trimming current stocks.

To convince Clarinda's CEO, Marco plans to perform a demonstration inventory analysis that focuses on the forms used by the surgical intensive care unit (SICU). Different forms are required for almost every aspect of SICU operations, including records of patient progress; requests for lab tests, blood products, and medications; nurse and physician notes; and transfer/discharge instructions. Exhibit 29.2 shows inventory usage and cost data on the SICU's 25 forms. To begin his demonstration analysis, Marco plans to conduct a new ABC analysis on the SICU's inventory. (Clarinda is in the process of converting to web-based forms as part of the transition to electronic medical records, but the paper forms will still be used for several years.)

As part of its commitment to supporting the local economy, Clarinda currently uses a single local source for all of the SICU's forms: Atwood Printing and Office Supplies (Supplier A). Supplier A requires a \$25 setup fee on each order, in addition to the cost per unit. Clarinda is considering using a national supplier, Bateman Medical Office Products (Supplier B), which charges no setup fee but does charge \$50 to cover postage and handling. Supplier B takes three days to deliver the forms, as opposed to only one day for Supplier A. Processing each order will cost Clarinda another \$25, regardless of which supplier is used. Thus, the total order cost is \$50 for Supplier A and \$75 for Supplier B.

Marco's ultimate goal is to use economic ordering quantity (EOQ) concepts to select the supplier for all forms used by the SICU. His primary areas of concern are (1) the number of orders placed each year, (2) reorder points (in units), and (3) total inventory costs. As part of the demonstration analysis, Marco will focus on the form used to order blood products from Clarinda's blood bank (SKU number 53104 in exhibit 28.2). The data associated with Suppliers A and B, as well as the inventory carrying costs and other data, are summarized in exhibit 29.3.

In addition to an analysis without safety stocks, Marco is concerned about the impact of safety stocks on the decision. Clarinda currently carries a safety stock of two units of SKU 53104 to protect itself against stockouts as a result of delivery delays or an increase in the usage rate (or both). When asked how that amount was calculated, the manager of the SICU stated that she didn't know but the hospital had always done it that way. However, if Clarinda decides to switch to Supplier B, the manager stated that it seems logical to increase the safety stock to six units to reflect Supplier B's three-times-as-long lead time. The following are of particular interest: the impact of safety stocks on inventory costs, the safety margins that such stocks would provide against higher-than-expected usage and shipping delays, and whether the current lead time for Supplier A and the estimate for Supplier B make any sense.

Marco has heard a rumor that Supplier B is about to offer a 10 percent discount if the entire year's demand (92 units) is ordered at once. He wants to know what the impact of this discount would be on the decision about which supplier to use. How high a discount is needed to make Supplier B less costly than Supplier A is also useful to know.

Furthermore, Marco is aware that the forms would not likely be ordered exactly as prescribed by the EOQ model, so he would like to know the impact of ordering variations on total inventory costs. Finally, he knows that Clarinda's CEO has expressed some doubt about the value of the EOQ model in making real-world inventory decisions. "If I'm right in my concerns," he asked, "what other inventory control methods are available to us?"

Place yourself in Marco's shoes to see if you can conduct the demonstration analysis that he has in mind.

EXHIBIT 29.1
ABC Classification Guidance

Classification	*Inventory Value*	*Inventory Amount*
A	60%–70%	10%–20%
B	20%–30%	30%–40%
C	10%–20%	50%–60%

EXHIBIT 29.2
Clarinda Community Hospital: Form Inventory Data for SICU

SKU Number	*Unit Size*	*Supplier A Unit Cost*	*Units Used Annually*
50071	25	$ 31	3
50083	25	16	4
50084	50	18	14
50091	250	86	28
50100	25	22	4
50102	250	793	3
50122	250	196	2
50129	250	177	3
50131	100	122	5
50132	100	98	5
50138	100	26	9
50139	50	21	10
50170	100	8	83
50172	100	44	4
50174	500	62	8
50193	25	2	66
50194	100	122	2
50206	250	11	279
50472	100	192	2
50475	125	551	4
50694	100	18	10
51060	100	102	6
53006	50	17	4
53104	50	66	92
57134	100	16	5

EXHIBIT 29.3
Clarinda Community Hospital Cost and Usage Data: Blood Product Ordering Form (SKU 53104)

Expected annual usage	92 units
Cost per Unit	
Supplier A	$66
Supplier B	$60
Inventory Carrying Costs	
Depreciation	0.0%
Storage and handling	17.1
Interest expense	6.6
Property taxes	0.4
Insurance	0.9
Total carrying costs	25.0%
Inventory Ordering Costs	
Supplier A	$50
Supplier B	$75
Current Safety Stocks	
Supplier A	2 units
Supplier B (estimate)	6 units
Delivery Times	
Supplier A	1 day
Supplier B	3 days

CASE 30

MILWAUKEE REGIONAL HEALTH SYSTEM

REVENUE CYCLE MANAGEMENT

ANDREW MAE HAS recently been hired as the vice president of revenue cycle management for the Milwaukee Regional Health System (MRHS), an integrated system with approximately $2.5 billion in annual revenues. Located in the Milwaukee, Wisconsin, metropolitan area, MRHS consists of an academic medical center, two community hospitals, and 30 outpatient primary and specialty care clinics. Annually, the hospitals collectively see more than 40,000 admissions, approximately 100,000 emergency department visits, and nearly 1 million outpatient encounters, while the clinics receive more than 1.6 million visits.

The vice president of revenue cycle management is a newly created position at MRHS. In that role, Andrew will oversee the merger of the currently separate hospital and physician revenue cycle departments. Andrew has been directed by MRHS's CEO to accomplish two primary goals: (1) lower the overall costs of revenue cycle management and (2) improve the revenue cycle process. (For more information on revenue cycle management, see the Healthcare Financial Management Association website at www.hfma.org or the Medical Group Management Association website at www.mgma.com. Search the term *revenue cycle* at both websites.)

Andrew understands that the first step in merging MRHS's separate revenue cycle departments is to alter the current perception that hospital and physician practice revenue cycles are inherently different. His goal in this regard is to illustrate the similarities and interdependencies among the revenue cycle processes to highlight what he believes to be the true determinants of revenue cycle success: (1) the collective hospital, physician, and revenue cycle staffs' effort to limit defects in the process and (2) the ability to identify, bill, and collect the correct net realizable value of each encounter. When asked about these statements, he explained that defects can be thought of as problems that impede the revenue cycle process, and net realizable value is the actual dollar amount expected to be collected from both patient and insurer for each service provided.

To begin the effort, Andrew prepared an orientation presentation for hospital and physician leadership on the integrated revenue cycle management process. Following is part of that presentation:

> The revenue cycle management process in healthcare provider organizations represents the process of identifying and securing the financial integrity of all services and care provided by the organization. It encompasses the information systems, policies, and methodologies used by an organization to review patients' and insurers' financial responsibilities, document the services and care provided, translate those activities to the appropriate billing amounts, issue invoices, and collect the correct payments. The revenue cycle management process also includes the evaluation of receivables (outstanding balances due for services provided) and the continuous review of the contract and auditing functions to ensure that all actions are in compliance with MRHS's hundreds of third-party payer contracts.
>
> The following schematic presents an overview of a typical provider revenue cycle management process as described by the Medical Group Management Association. It is followed by a brief description of each function and the information gathered within the function, beginning with scheduling, which typically begins the revenue cycle process. Some potential defects that can occur within each function are also listed. It is important to understand that immediate identification and correction of defects are critical to good revenue cycle performance because they can create bottlenecks, require reprocessing, result in poor patient experiences, and/or reduce net realizable values.

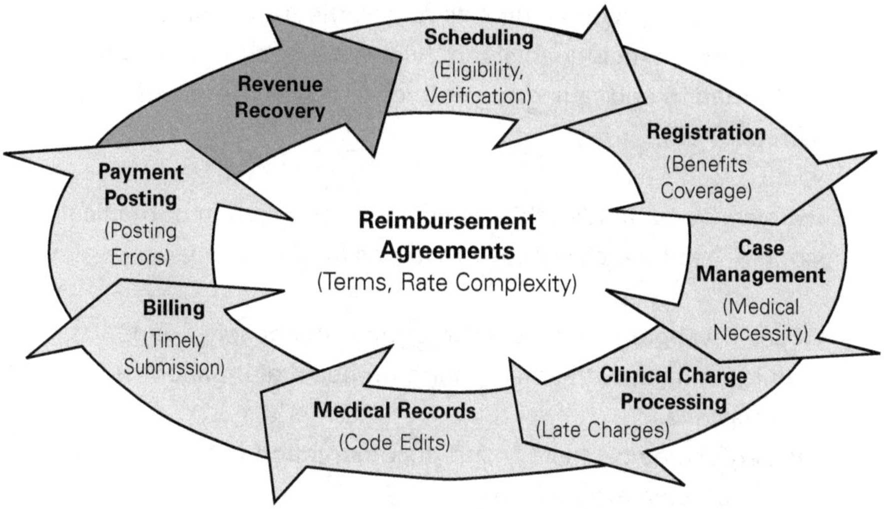

Scheduling. Typically, this function is the first interaction between the patient and the provider system. Hence, scheduling represents the beginning of the revenue cycle process.

- Scheduling occurs throughout the hospital and clinic settings; emergency department and walk-in patients require unique scheduling procedures.
- Patient information gathering begins with the description of the health issue/care need and type of insurance coverage.
- Examples of potential defects during the execution of this function include directing patients to the wrong service and failing to properly identify and verify insurance coverage and obtain precertification (if required).

Registration. This is the first patient experience on the first day of each patient encounter.

- Registration occurs throughout the hospital and clinic settings.
- Patient information gathered in the scheduling process is confirmed or updated, and additional health condition and financial/insurance information is obtained if needed.

- Examples of potential defects during the execution of this function include misidentifying patient and/or insurer information and failing to verify coverage and precertification (if required).

Case management. With this function, the translation of medically necessary healthcare services to charges for those services begins.

- Case management occurs throughout the hospital and clinic settings, with an emphasis on hospital inpatient admissions.
- Patients' medical history and documentation of current status and care plan are reviewed.
- Examples of potential defects during the execution of this function include ordering or performing services that are not preauthorized or are deemed medically unnecessary by the insurer.

Clinical charge processing. Here, the clinical documentation of services provided is translated to line-item charges.

- Clinical charge processing, which applies to hospital and clinic services, uses diagnosis-related group (DRG) and revenue codes for hospital billing and Current Procedural Terminology (CPT) and Healthcare Common Procedure Coding System codes for outpatient and physician billing.
- Documentation of all services and the level of care provided is matched to the charge description master (chargemaster) file.
- Examples of potential defects during the execution of this function include charges submitted after the allowed documentation period (late charges) and improper matching of clinical entries with the chargemaster file.

Medical records. This function consists of the systematic compilation and documentation of all care provided to patients during and, if appropriate, subsequent to the encounter.

- A single patient record for all services is created.

- Information in the record is available to patients and other care providers, subject to certain regulations and restrictions.
- Examples of potential defects during the execution of this function include documentation and coding errors and lag times in the coding and compiling of the record (discharged but not billed).

Billing. This function converts the information gathered in previous functions to patient and insurer bills (invoices).

- In the billing function, Centers for Medicare & Medicaid Services (CMS) UB-04 forms (for hospital inpatient and outpatient insurance billing) and CMS 1500 forms (for physician insurance billing) are prepared.
- Given the highly technical nature of the UB-04 and CMS 1500 forms, separate billing statements are created for patients that indicate their payment responsibilities.
- Examples of potential defects during the execution of this function include a lack of timely bill submission and failure to follow the specific billing rules required by the insurer, which results in payment denials.

Payment posting. In this function, the accounts receivable entry is adjusted as invoices are collected. Note that this process may require a coordinated effort of follow-up and collections actions directed at the insurer or patient or both.

- Payment posting is complicated by the many different rules, regulations, and data formats required by private and government insurers.
- Unpaid balances due from patients undergo another round of processing, including research to find additional insurance and/or financial status information.
- Examples of potential defects during the execution of this function include mishandling of insurer payment denials, posting errors that misstate the remaining outstanding balance from patients, and patients' confusion over insurer invoicing and coverage.

Revenue recovery. This audit function takes place continuously to examine the entire revenue cycle process. The following steps are taken during revenue recovery:

- Measure the performance of each revenue cycle function according to established benchmarks.
- Identify the cause of each defect and take corrective action as necessary.
- Ensure compliance with regulatory requirements and confirm that payments received are consistent with all insurer contract provisions and the organization's charity care policy.
- Defects that can occur in this function include improper selection of benchmark metrics or values and failure to aggressively audit or correct defects in the revenue cycle.

The hospital and physician leaders found Andrew's presentation to be a valuable overview of the revenue cycle process. However, they remained concerned over the merging of the two revenue cycle departments and questioned the metrics chosen to monitor performance. In addition, they expressed a need to know more about the concept of defects and the ways to identify and correct them. Finally, the leaders wanted to learn more about net realizable value—specifically, the differences across the most important insurer contracts. To address these issues, Andrew began to create two documents: one that includes both hospital and clinic revenue cycle performance metrics and one that highlights the differences in reimbursement methodologies and net realizable values. **Note that all metric and reimbursement values provided in this case are for instructional use only and should not be used for other purposes.**

The next meeting with hospital and physician leadership is scheduled in two weeks, and Andrew had planned to complete the two projects before then. Unfortunately, he broke his leg in a snowmobile accident and requires surgery and a short hospitalization, so he is unable to get the work done in time for the meeting. Thus, he has asked you, an administrative fellow at MRHS, to help out with the following three tasks:

1. Establish two overall revenue cycle performance metrics and one defect metric for each revenue cycle function, from scheduling through payment posting. The metrics should be

based on nationally accepted practices, and the list should include definitions and current benchmark values. Andrew has already started this task, so he provided you with a template, as shown in exhibit 30.1, that contains one overall performance metric—accounts receivable (A/R) days—that is already filled in. In addition, he finished compiling a list of metric candidates and benchmark values from various sources, which is provided in exhibit 30.2. Thus, your task is to choose one additional overall performance metric and the single best defect metric for each function listed in exhibit 30.1 for both the hospital and clinic settings. Andrew mentioned that there will be a great deal of discussion of these metrics at the meeting, so it is essential that you fully justify your selections.

2. Compare the MRHS actual values for the metrics chosen, provided in exhibit 30.3, with the benchmark values. Discuss the implications of your comparisons and, most important, suggest the corrective actions that should be implemented to bring MRHS in line with national standards for the areas of subpar performance.
3. Perform an extensive pricing study comparing MRHS's gross charges (chargemaster prices) with those of other healthcare providers in its market to competitively align its price structure. Of course, MRHS typically gets paid far less than gross charges for the care it provides. The actual billing amount is determined by analyzing the hundreds of reimbursement contracts MRHS has with insurers and policies that MRHS has in place for low-income patients. (For more information about chargemaster pricing, refer to "The Pricing of U.S. Hospital Services: Chaos Behind a Veil of Secrecy," by Uwe E. Reinhardt, posted at www.healthaffairs.org/doi/10.1377/hlthaff.25.1.57).

Andrew wants to highlight the role that contract provisions with insurers play in determining the final reimbursement amount. Thus, he has asked you to calculate the expected total reimbursement amount according to gross (chargemaster) prices, the reimbursement model used, and the actual collections experience for two common procedures: CPT 73722 (magnetic resonance imaging [MRI] of the knee) and DRG 470 (major joint replacement). To help you, he created the template in exhibit 30.4, with one cell completed. After you finish the table, he would like you to assess the fairness and efficiency of the current fragmented payment system to providers, insurers, patients, and society (the ultimate bearers of healthcare costs). In addition, you have been asked to calculate the average expected payment for the MRI and joint replacement procedures. MRHS's payer mix is 46 percent Medicare, 34 percent commercial/managed care, 16 percent Medicaid, and 4 percent self-pay/no insurance.

EXHIBIT 30.1
Benchmarking Template

	Metric	*Metric Definition*	*Hospital Benchmark*	*Clinic Benchmark*
Overall Metrics	A/R days	Net patient accounts receivable/(Annual patient service revenue/365 days)	48.3 days	28.5 days
Defect Metrics				
Scheduling				
Registration				
Case management				
Clinical charge processing				
Medical records				
Billing				
Payment posting				

EXHIBIT 30.2 Selected National Benchmark Data

	Metric Definition	*Hospital Benchmark*	*Clinic Benchmark*
Overall Metrics			
A/R days	Net patient accounts receivable/ (Annual net patient revenue/365 days)	48.3 days	28.5 days
Percent of A/R greater than 90 days	Accounts receivable aged greater than 90 days/Total accounts receivable	29.6%	19.0%
Cost to collect	Total revenue cycle costs/ Total cash collected	3.5%	4.2%
Defect Metrics			
Scheduling			
Preregistration rate	No. of patient encounters preregistered/ No. of scheduled patient encounters	84.8%	99.1%
Insurance verification rate	No. of verified encounters/ No. of registered encounters	90.0%	98.7%
Registration			
Point-of-service collection rate	Point-of-service cash collections/ Total patient cash collected	13.4%	36.2%
Registration quality score	No. of correct patient demographic and insurance data elements input/ Total data elements required at registration	98.7%	99.4%
Case management			
Preauthorization denial rate	No. of claims denied for no preauthorization/ No. of claims submitted	1.8%	0.7%
Percent of medical necessity write-offs	Medical necessity write-offs/Total charges	0.4%	0.6%
Clinical charge processing			
Charge lag days	Days between service date and posting of charge/Encounters billed	3.6 days	5.1 days
Late charge %	Charges posted more than 3 days after the date of service/Total charges	8.4%	78.6%

(continued)

EXHIBIT 30.2 Selected National Benchmark Data (continued)

	Metric Definition	Hospital Benchmark	Clinic Benchmark
Medical records			
Days in total discharged not final billed	Gross dollars in accounts receivable unbilled/(Annual net patient revenue/365 days)	7.4 days	5.9 days
Coding quality score	No. of correct coding data elements input/Total data elements required at coding	96.5%	93.2%
Billing			
Initial denial rate	No. of claims denied/No. of claims submitted	4.9%	8.2%
Clean claim rate	No. of claims that pass edits with no manual intervention/Total billed claims	76.8%	81.2%
Payment posting			
Percent of payments posted electronically	Dollars posted electronically/Total payments posted	86.7%	83.1%
Net days revenue in credit balance[a]	Dollars in credit balance/(Annual net patient revenue/365 days)	1.9 days	3.2 days

[a]Credit balance reflects monies owed to payers because of improper billing.

EXHIBIT 30.3
Selected MRHS Metric Values

	MRHS Hospitals	*MRHS Clinics*
Overall Metrics		
A/R days	45.4 days	26.3 days
% of A/R greater than 90 days	21.5%	20.1%
Cost to collect	2.9%	4.5%
Defect Metrics		
Scheduling		
Preregistration rate	80.8%	99.9%
Insurance verification rate	85.3%	100.0%
Registration		
Point-of-service collection rate	8.7%	48.5%
Registration quality score	91.6%	99.9%
Case management		
Preauthorization denial rate	2.4%	0.3%
Percent of medical necessity write-offs	0.7%	0.2%
Clinical charge processing		
Charge lag days	3.2 days	6.8 days
Late charge percent	2.1%	86.9%
Medical records		
Days in total discharged not final billed	4.5 days	7.5 days
Coding quality score	98.7%	90.2%
Billing		
Initial denial rate	5.6%	7.8%
Clean claim rate	72.4%	85.2%
Payment posting		
Percent of payments posted electronically	90.1%	78.9%
Net days revenue in credit balance	2.5 days	2.3 days

EXHIBIT 30.4
Calculation Templates

	MRI of the Knee CPT 73722 Charge = $2,800	*Major Joint Replacement (4-day LOS) DRG 470 Charge = $50,000*
Medicare		
Base payment rate	$341.61	$17,955.00
No-payment denial rate of 3%	(10.25)	
Part A deductible of $1,184 @ 65% collection rate	N/A	
Part B deductible of $140 @ 78% collection rate	(30.80)	
Total reimbursement	$300.56	
Medicaid		
Per diem of $284/visit or $2,044/day		
No-payment denial rate of 0.5%		
Total reimbursement		
Commercial/managed care		
58% of charge		
No-payment denial rate of 12%		
20% patient coinsurance @ 40% collection rate		
Total reimbursement		
Self-pay/no insurance		
30% discount		
5% self-pay collection rate		
Total reimbursement		

CPT: Current Procedural Terminology; DRG: diagnosis-related group

Hint: All of the data needed to complete this table are listed on the template labels. Note that the chargemaster price for each procedure and the length of stay (LOS) for the joint replacement are listed in the column header information. In addition, remember that Medicare Part A pays for inpatient services (e.g., joint replacements), whereas Part B pays for outpatient services (e.g., MRIs).

PART

BUSINESS VALUATION

XI

CASE

31

ST. BENEDICT'S TEACHING HOSPITAL

MERGER ANALYSIS

THE PATIENT BASE of Lafayette County, Indiana, is currently served by three hospitals: (1) St. Benedict's Teaching Hospital, a not-for-profit, university-related hospital with 525 beds; (2) Wabash Regional Medical Center, a 250-bed, for-profit hospital owned by Hospital Associates of America (HAA), a national chain; and (3) Lafayette General, a 400-bed, not-for-profit, acute care hospital owned by Hoosier Healthcare. St. Benedict's and Lafayette General are located less than one mile from one another, while Wabash Regional is about five miles away from St. Benedict's, in a newer and more rapidly developing section of the county.

The service area has a total of 1,175 licensed beds, or about 3.5 beds per 1,000 population, which is higher than the national average of about 2.4 beds per 1,000 and much higher than the roughly 2 beds per 1,000 needed under an aggressive utilization management program. Of course, as a tertiary care facility, St. Benedict's receives patients from throughout the state, but the bulk of its patients still come from the local five-county area.

With an excess of hospital beds in the service area, the status quo may not survive the changing healthcare environment. Indeed, Lafayette General has had some tough years recently, as evidenced by its number of discharges, which have fallen to 11,412 in 2021 from 12,055 in 2020 and 12,824 in 2019. In addition, HAA has been aggressive in building market share in other areas of Indiana through both acquisitions and hospital expansions. With these factors in place, some consolidation in the local hospital market will likely take place, and the most likely result is the acquisition of Lafayette General by either St. Benedict's or HAA.

Lafayette General operated as a county hospital for more than 50 years and hence developed a reputation for providing healthcare services to low-income residents. After many years of operating losses, the county concluded that it could no longer afford to operate the hospital. In 1987, the county sold the hospital for $1 to Hoosier Healthcare, a not-for-profit managed care organization and provider, which by 2021 had become the state's largest integrated healthcare company.

Hoosier Healthcare's major business line is managed care. Its numerous plans, including health maintenance organization, preferred provider organization, point of service, and Medicare and Medicaid plans, serve more than 1 million members in 25 Indiana counties, encompassing all the state's major metropolitan areas. In addition to managed care plans, Hoosier Healthcare owns seven different providers: two acute care hospitals (including Lafayette General), one rehabilitation hospital, one mental health facility, one hospice, one home health care agency, and one retirement community.

Lafayette General is the flagship of Hoosier Healthcare's provider network, and the company has kept the hospital in excellent condition in spite of falling inpatient utilization. In fact, Lafayette General recently built the state-of-the-art HeartCare Center and the modern MaternityCare Center. Furthermore, Lafayette General operates a full-service emergency department and a medical helicopter service.

In response to the current situation, St. Benedict's has formed a special committee to consider the feasibility of making an offer to Hoosier Healthcare to acquire Lafayette General. The committee's primary goals are as follows:

1. To place a dollar value on Lafayette General's equity (fund) capital, assuming that the hospital will be acquired and operated by St. Benedict's
2. To develop a financing plan for the acquisition

In addition, the committee has been asked to consider two other issues related to the potential acquisition:

1. What is the best organizational structure for a combined enterprise? Currently, both Lafayette General and St. Benedict's have separate boards of directors and management staffs. Of

course, currently the senior members of the Lafayette General board are also Hoosier Healthcare officers.

2. Should the medical staffs of the two hospitals be integrated, and, if so, in what way? The medical staff of Lafayette General consists of local physicians, including many family practice physicians, whereas the medical staff at St. Benedict's is almost entirely made up of specialists, and all are members of the local university's college of medicine with responsibilities that go well beyond clinical practice.

A new committee will be formed to finalize recommendations on these issues should St. Benedict's management agree to move forward with the acquisition offer, but some preliminary judgments are needed at this time. As a starting point in the valuation analysis, the committee has obtained historical income statement and balance sheet data on both hospitals. Exhibit 31.1 contains the data for Lafayette General, and exhibit 31.2 provides the data for St. Benedict's. Both sets of statements are abbreviated but contain the data considered to be most relevant to the analysis. In addition, relevant comparative data are presented in exhibit 31.3 and relevant market data are shown in exhibit 31.4. (Assume that the data in exhibits 31.3 and 31.4 reflect late-2021 conditions.)

One of the toughest tasks that the committee faces is the development of Lafayette General's pro forma (forecasted) cash flow statements, which form the basis of the discounted cash flow valuation. Several basic questions must be answered before any numbers can be generated. First, what synergies, if any, can be realized from the merger, and how long will it take for such synergies to develop? For example, can duplications be eliminated? Both hospitals have "mercy flight" helicopters and offer full emergency department services, even though the two hospitals are only one mile apart. What is the impact of such operational changes on revenues and costs and hence on the net cash flows that Lafayette General's assets can produce? Second, once the consolidation takes place and all synergies have been realized, what is the long-term growth prospect for Lafayette General's cash flows? Third, what impact would the acquisition have on St. Benedict's own cash flows? Any change in St. Benedict's revenues or costs that results from the acquisition must be included in the analysis. The answers to these questions and others form the basis for the pro forma cash flow statements.

You are the chair of the special committee formed at St. Benedict's to evaluate the potential acquisition. You must present your findings and recommendations to the hospital's board of directors. Because the case contains far less information than normally available in a merger analysis, especially when the potential merger is friendly, you must make many difficult assumptions to complete your analysis. Although you do not know much about Lafayette General's local market, you do know the current trends in the healthcare industry. Use this knowledge to help make judgments about the case. The quality of many, if not most, real-world financial analyses depends more on the validity of the underlying assumptions than on the theoretical "correctness" of the analytical techniques.

Note that there is no preferred solution to this case, so your case analysis will be judged as much on the assumptions used in the analysis as on the analysis itself. Finally, remember that numerous risk analysis techniques are available that can be used to give decision makers some feel for the risks involved.

EXHIBIT 31.1
Lafayette General: Historical Financial Statements (in Millions of Dollars)

	2017	2018	2019	2020	2021
Income Statements					
Inpatient revenue	$ 42.472	$ 46.014	$ 53.410	$ 58.650	$ 59.513
Outpatient revenue	28.314	30.676	35.606	39.100	39.675
Net patient service revenue	$ 70.786	$ 76.690	$ 89.016	$ 97.750	$ 99.188
Nonoperating revenue	1.922	1.515	1.367	1.725	1.048
Total revenues	$ 72.708	$ 78.205	$ 90.383	$ 99.475	$100.236
Patient services expenses	$ 60.245	$ 73.858	$ 81.525	$ 90.645	$ 89.505
Interest expense	3.045	3.147	3.093	3.002	2.980
Depreciation	3.466	3.689	4.395	4.258	6.031
Total expenses	$ 66.756	$ 80.694	$ 89.013	$ 97.905	$ 98.516
Net income	$ 5.952	($ 2.489)	$ 1.370	$ 1.570	$ 1.720
Balance Sheets					
Cash and investments	$ 2.388	$ 1.538	$ 0.162	$ 0.185	$ 0.198
Accounts receivable	18.860	20.581	20.821	21.570	16.732
Other current assets	4.539	8.475	4.669	2.585	2.898
Total current assets	$ 25.787	$ 30.594	$ 25.652	$ 24.340	$ 19.828
Gross plant and equipment	$102.596	$116.694	$122.611	$133.499	$146.130
Accumulated depreciation	27.243	30.505	34.900	39.158	45.189
Net plant and equipment	$ 75.353	$ 86.189	$ 87.711	$ 94.341	$100.941
Total assets	$101.140	$116.783	$113.363	$118.681	$120.769
Current liabilities	$ 9.182	$ 13.584	$ 5.771	$ 10.689	$ 11.431
Long-term debt	33.572	47.302	50.325	49.155	48.781
Total liabilities	$ 42.754	$ 60.886	$ 56.096	$ 59.844	$ 60.212
Fund balance	58.386	55.897	57.267	58.837	60.557
Total claims	$101.140	$116.783	$113.363	$118.681	$120.769

EXHIBIT 31.2
St. Benedict's Teaching Hospital: Historical Financial Statements (in Millions of Dollars)

	2017	2018	2019	2020	2021
Income Statements					
Inpatient revenue	$170.195	$198.137	$221.826	$226.944	$251.935
Outpatient revenue	34.225	39.517	46.828	56.226	65.507
Net patient service revenue	$204.420	$237.654	$268.654	$283.170	$317.442
Nonoperating revenue	5.587	8.899	12.193	22.672	9.979
Total revenues	$210.007	$246.553	$280.847	$305.842	$327.421
Patient services expenses	$178.788	$207.596	$231.673	$254.704	$277.938
Interest expense	9.232	10.468	11.983	10.691	9.997
Depreciation	13.289	16.637	19.621	23.286	26.489
Total expenses	$201.309	$234.701	$263.277	$288.681	$314.424
Net income	$ 8.698	$ 11.852	$ 17.570	$ 17.161	$ 12.997
Balance Sheets					
Cash and investments	$ 17.918	$ 19.862	$ 24.660	$ 27.726	$ 25.220
Accounts receivable	66.212	72.989	99.867	100.297	97.494
Other current assets	12.315	16.771	20.741	20.542	22.757
Total current assets	$ 96.445	$109.622	$145.268	$148.565	$145.471
Gross plant and equipment	$348.288	$341.064	$335.313	$362.152	$400.546
Accumulated depreciation	75.139	76.575	90.056	109.468	123.567
Net plant and equipment	$273.149	$264.489	$245.257	$252.684	$276.979
Total assets	$369.594	$374.111	$390.525	$401.249	$422.450
Current liabilities	$ 42.437	$ 35.061	$ 39.511	$ 37.733	$ 39.817
Long-term debt	146.997	147.038	141.432	136.773	142.893
Total liabilities	$189.434	$182.099	$180.943	$174.506	$182.710
Fund balance	180.160	192.012	209.582	226.743	239.740
Total claims	$369.594	$374.111	$390.525	$401.249	$422.450

Note: The hospital's current target cash balance is $5 million.

EXHIBIT 31.3
Selected Comparative Data

	Lafayette	*St. Benedict's*
Average age of plant	6.8 years	8.5 years
Licensed beds	400	525
Occupancy rate	52.7%	64.2%
Average length of stay	5.5 days	6.6 days
Number of discharges	11,412	19,748
Medicare percent	57.2%	29.7%
Medicaid percent	10.3%	13.0%
Medicare case mix index	1.51	2.13
Gross price per discharge	$11,688	$20,204
Net price per discharge	$5,850	$12,757
Cost per discharge	$5,703	$12,144

EXHIBIT 31.4
Selected Market and Hospital Data

US Treasury Yield Curve

Maturity	*Interest Rate*
6 months	3.0%
1 year	3.5
5 years	3.9
10 years	4.5
20 years	5.0
30 years	5.1

Market Risk Premium

Historical risk premium	7.0%
Average current risk premium as forecasted by three investment banking firms	6.0%

Market Betas, Capitalization, and Tax Rates of Two Publicly Traded Hospital Companies

Company	*Beta*	*Debt/Asset Ratio*	*Tax Rate*
Provident Healthcare	1.1	50%	30%
National Health Company	1.2	65%	30%

(continued)

EXHIBIT 31.4
Selected Market and Hospital Data (continued)

Ratio of Stock Price to EBITDA per Share

Provident Healthcare	8.5
National Health Company	7.5

Ratio of Total Equity Market Value to Number of Discharges

Provident Healthcare	$8,000
National Health Company	$7,000

Proportion of Cash to Current Assets

Large hospital average	5.0%

Days Cash on Hand

Large hospital average	22 days
St. Benedict's	31 days

EBITDA: Earnings before interest, taxes, depreciation, and amortization

Note: The data in this exhibit are for use in this case only and do not necessarily reflect current market data.

CASE 32

BEACHSIDE HEALTH PARTNERS

JOINT VENTURE ANALYSIS

BEACHSIDE HOSPITAL IS a 320-bed, acute care, not-for-profit hospital located in Myrtle Beach, South Carolina. It is well known as a leader in new technology and hence draws patients from as far away as Georgetown, South Carolina, to the south and Wilmington, North Carolina, to the north. Beachside contracts with the Grand Strand Radiology Group to provide radiology services for its patients. Basically, Beachside furnishes the radiology equipment and technicians and performs the tests, while the Grand Strand physicians read the results. Because Grand Strand bills patients separately for the readings, there is no direct payment from Beachside to Grand Strand.

At the end of a monthly medical staff meeting, Dr. George Brigham, head of Grand Strand, presented a proposal to Mary Cohen, Beachside's CEO. Grand Strand wants to form a partnership with Beachside to provide renal diagnostic and treatment services, primarily lithotripsy and ureteroscopy.

- Lithotripsy uses a lithotripter, equipment that sends high-energy shock waves, guided by X-ray or ultrasound, to break up stones in the kidney, bladder, or ureter (duct connecting the kidneys and the bladder). During the procedure, patients lie on a water-filled cushion placed on the examination table and are given general anesthesia to keep them asleep and pain free. Shock or sound waves shatter the stones into pieces small enough to pass out of the body in urine. This procedure takes about 45 minutes to 1 hour (https://medlineplus.gov/ency/article/007113.htm).

- Ureteroscopy uses a ureteroscope, a long, thin device attached to a tiny light and camera, to inspect the ureter for abnormalities. This tool also carries tiny instruments that remove or break up kidney stones or place stents that aid in passing kidney stones or urine. General anesthesia is administered to patients before the procedure, which usually takes about an hour (https://medlineplus.gov/ency/article/007593.htm).

In total, the capital cost of the lithotripter and ureteroscope is approximately $1 million.

The idea of a partnership with Grand Strand, even if it lasts only two years, appeals to Mary. First, by offering lithotripsy and ureteroscopy, Beachside is reinforcing its position as the regional leader in renal health. Second, the partnership would position Beachside as the leading provider in the competitive Myrtle Beach market. Mary believes Beachside's board of trustees would not be willing to bear the entire risk of the equipment purchase but might be willing to go along with a joint venture. Thus, she asked Dr. Brigham to look into the matter further and develop a specific joint venture proposal.

Mary had almost forgotten the matter when, two months later, Dr. Brigham appeared with the following joint venture proposal (exhibit 32.1 contains a summary of the proposed financing):

1. A separate business entity, Beachside Health Partners (the Partnership), would be formed.
2. The Partnership would have two general partners: Grand Strand and Beachside. Grand Strand would put up $300,000 in capital and retain 60 percent management control, whereas Beachside would furnish $200,000 in capital and obtain 40 percent control. (Grand Strand is incorporated, but it files federal income taxes as an S corporation. It would incorporate a subsidiary S corporation for the sole purpose of investing in the Partnership. S corporations pay no federal income taxes. Rather, as in a partnership, the income is constructively prorated among the owners and taxed as ordinary income.)
3. Twenty-five limited partnerships would be offered to local physicians for $20,000 each. The limited partners would have no liability beyond their $20,000 investments but would have no

control rights, either. (The Partnership is purposely restricted to 25 limited partners because a larger number would require a more complicated partnership registration procedure with the state of South Carolina.)

4. An additional $1 million would be obtained from South Carolina Bancorp in the form of a five-year term (amortized) loan carrying an interest rate of 8 percent. The bank would require the Partnership to pledge the equipment as collateral for the loan. In the event of default by the Partnership, the market value of the equipment would first be used to offset the principal balance, and then Grand Strand would be liable for 60 percent and Beachside for 40 percent of any remaining balance.

The $2 million initial capital infusion would be sufficient to purchase and install the lithotripter and ureteroscope as well as to pay the consulting, legal, and accounting costs associated with forming the Partnership. Beachside would lease the Partnership the space for the equipment, furnish the technical support required to operate the equipment, and handle billing and collections. Of course, all services provided to the Partnership by Beachside would be handled at arm's length, and hence the Partnership would pay Beachside prevailing market rates for the services provided.

The Partnership itself would not be taxed, but its distributions represent income and as such would be taxed on the basis of each partner's tax status. The distributions to Beachside would be nontaxable because the joint venture is consistent with Beachside's not-for-profit status. The distributions to Grand Strand and to the limited partners would be taxed as ordinary income. However, about 50 percent of the distributions would represent a return of capital (depreciation cash flow), which is not taxed; hence, taxable investors would pay taxes at an effective rate of only about 20 percent.

The cash flows from the Partnership would be distributed according to the following plan:

1. The Partnership would distribute all earned net cash flow to the partners at the end of each year.
2. At the end of the first year, the general partners would receive 30 percent of the cash flow and the limited partners would receive 70 percent. Following the distribution at the end of each year, the total accumulated dollar return provided to the limited partners

would be calculated. If this amount is less than the limited partners' total investment, the limited partners would continue to receive 70 percent of the cash flow in the following year.

3. In the years after the year in which the limited partners recover their initial investment, 50 percent of the cash flow would be distributed to the general partners, while 50 percent would go to the limited partners.
4. The cash flow allocated to the general partners would be distributed proportionally to Grand Strand and to Beachside on the basis of each partner's relative investment: 60 percent would go to Grand Strand and 40 percent to Beachside.

The key to a sound financial analysis is good cash flow estimates. Mary and Dr. Brigham devoted an entire day to the cash flow estimation process, and many other individuals provided input. If the joint venture gets off the ground, the lithotripter and ureteroscope would be in operation by the end of the year (Year 0). Both pieces of equipment would be available for 50 weeks each year, and the best estimate is that four procedures would be performed per week during the first year (Year 1).

Based on discussions with selected payers, the Partnership is expected to receive $5,000 per procedure on average. Thus, the net revenue in Year 1 is forecasted to be 4(50)($5,000) = $1,000,000. Physician and public awareness would increase after the first year, and hence volume is projected to increase to five procedures per week during Year 2. However, at least one competing hospital would likely have its own lithotripter and ureteroscope by this time; thus, volume is expected to fall back to four procedures per week in Year 3, to three procedures per week in Year 4, and to two procedures per week in Year 5.

The net revenue per procedure is approximately the same for lithotripsy and ureteroscopy. However, projecting the trend for net revenue per procedure is difficult. On the one hand, it might be possible to increase the charge for lithotripsy and ureteroscopy by the overall inflation rate, or even more. But on the other hand, Medicare and Medicaid patients would likely be an increasing part of the patient mix, and reimbursement for their care is often set well below chargemaster prices; indeed, such payments could be below costs. Because these factors tend to offset one another, no inflation adjustments will be applied to revenue estimates.

Technology is moving quickly in this area, so assessing whether the equipment would have an economic life of more than five years is difficult. For the same reason, estimating the equipment's salvage value at the end of five years is also difficult. Because of the uncertainties involved, Mary and Dr. Brigham agreed to assume a five-year life for the Partnership and a zero salvage value for the equipment.

Exhibit 32.2 contains the forecasted cash flow statements for the Partnership for Year 1 and Year 2. Note the following points:

1. Technician costs are estimated at $100 per procedure, so total technician support for Year 1 is (4)(50)$100 = $20,000.
2. Clerical costs are estimated at $50 per procedure, so total clerical expense for Year 1 is (4)(50)$50 = $10,000.
3. Technician and clerical salaries are expected to increase at an annual rate of 5 percent.
4. Rent, insurance, and marketing expenses are forecasted to be $15,000, $10,000, and $5,000, respectively, in Year 1. These costs are expected to increase at the projected inflation rate of 5 percent.
5. Expendable supplies are estimated to cost $25 per procedure, and hence the Year 1 total supplies cost is (4)(50)$25 = $5,000. The cost of expendables is expected to increase at the 5 percent inflation rate, and usage is increasing as well.
6. The service contract on both pieces of equipment is expected to cost $50,000 in Year 1 and Year 2, $75,000 in Year 3 and Year 4, and $100,000 in Year 5. These costs grow over time because cumulative usage increases the need for maintenance and parts replacement.
7. The Partnership must pay property taxes on both pieces of equipment, which are currently estimated to be $23,000 in Year 1, $24,000 in Year 2, $25,000 in Year 3, $26,000 in Year 4, and $27,000 in Year 5.
8. The Partnership's administrative expenses are estimated to be $30,000 in Year 1. These expenses consist of accounting and legal fees as well as reimbursement for management time spent on Partnership business. These costs are expected to increase at the 5 percent inflation rate.

9. Principal and interest expenses are based on annual amortization of an 8 percent, five-year loan of $1,000,000.
10. Miscellaneous expenses, which consist of the costs involved in the semiannual partners meeting, forms printing, expendable clerical supplies, and others, are expected to be a constant $20,000 over the next five years.

Mary and Dr. Brigham are most concerned about the estimates for weekly volume, and hence they spent a great deal of time developing the following data:

	Weekly Volume				
Case	*Year 1*	*Year 2*	*Year 3*	*Year 4*	*Year 5*
Worst	3	4	3	2	1
Most likely	4	5	4	3	2
Best	5	6	5	4	3

The most likely scenario assumes that a competing hospital would have its own lithotripter and ureteroscope by Year 3, the worst case assumes this would occur by Year 2, and the best case assumes this would occur by Year 4. The best estimates for the probabilities of the above scenarios are 25 percent for the best and worst cases and 50 percent for the most likely case.

The current yield on 20-year T-bonds is 5 percent. Furthermore, a local brokerage firm estimated the market risk premium to be 5 percentage points. Thus, according to the capital asset pricing model (CAPM), the current required rate of return on an average-risk (large publicly traded company with a beta equal to 1.0) stock investment is 10 percent.

In addition to the efficacy concerns, all parties have expressed concerns over two other issues. First, are there any indirect costs or benefits (that do not appear in the estimated cash flows) to any of the parties to the joint venture? Second, does the Partnership raise any legal or ethical issues for any of the parties?

You have been hired as a consultant to examine the feasibility of the proposed joint venture. You must assess the situation and prepare a report for Beachside and Grand Strand. Mary and Dr. Brigham know that the joint venture will never be successful unless all parties are satisfied with the financial arrangements. Thus, they believe that an impartial analysis should be conducted to assess the risk/return potential for each party. Furthermore, if any of the parties do not appear to be treated fairly under the initial proposal, they would seek recommendations that would increase overall fairness and hence give the proposal a better chance of success.

In beginning your analysis, you recognize that several different cash flow/discount rate formats are available for valuing businesses. In essence, the partnership analysis is merely business valuation—but from the perspective of different classes of equity participants. To allow the analysis to include multiple equity perspectives, it is necessary to structure the cash flows using the free-cash-flow-to-equity-holders method. Here, the focus is on the cash flows that are available for distribution to equity holders, so interest expense (and any other debt flows) must be subtracted from the cash flow stream. (Note that this format differs from a typical capital budgeting analysis, in which debt flows are not considered.) Because the estimated net cash flows are equity flows, they must be discounted by a cost of equity. (Typical capital budgeting cash flows are operating cash flows and hence are discounted by the corporate cost of capital, adjusted for individual project risk.)

You also note that sensitivity analysis is not useful in this situation because the unique cash flow distribution system confounds such an analysis. In addition, internal rate of return, although useful for the base case, breaks down in a scenario analysis because some scenarios create non-normal cash flows. Thus, you plan to use standard scenario analysis techniques for your risk analysis, with net present value as the profitability measure. Furthermore, because the purpose of scenario analysis is to assess risk, rather than incorporate it, you plan to use a constant 10 percent discount rate for all partners in the scenario analysis.

EXHIBIT 32.1
Beachside Health Partners: Partnership Financing Summary

Capital Contribution	General Partners	Limited Partners	Debt Financing
$ 300,000	Group		
200,000	Hospital		
500,000		25 @ $20,000 each	
1,000,000			SC Bancorp
$2,000,000			

EXHIBIT 32.2
Beachside Health Partners: Forecasted Cash Flow Statements

	Year 1	Year 2
Net revenues	$1,000,000	$1,250,000
Cash operating costs		
Technician support	$ 20,000	$ 26,250
Clerical support	10,000	13,125
Rent	15,000	15,750
Insurance	10,000	10,500
Marketing expenses	5,000	5,250
Expendable supplies	5,000	6,563
Service contract	50,000	50,000
Property taxes	23,000	24,000
Administrative expense	30,000	31,500
Principal repayment	170,456	184,093
Interest expense	80,000	66,363
Miscellaneous expenses	20,000	20,000
Total expenses	$ 438,456	$ 453,394
Partnership net cash flow	$ 561,544	$ 796,606

CASE 33

BEDFORD CLINICS

PRACTICE VALUATION

United Health Services Corporation

United Health Services Corporation (UHSC) is a large integrated healthcare business that serves northern and central California. In response to healthcare reform, UHSC has been acquiring primary care practices to capture market share. The basic competitive strategy has been to select geographically well-placed practices that will attract and retain patients. UHSC believes this strategy is critical in the shift to population health management.

Initial acquisitions were not entirely successful, primarily because of overvaluation of downstream revenue. In essence, UHSC overpaid for practices in anticipation of higher referrals and revenue after acquisition. Most of these practices were small, with only one physician. UHSC quickly learned that, typically, these practices had insufficient patient volume to cover the substantial fixed costs of running a practice, had a payer mix of more than half from less profitable Medicare and Medicaid sources, included a physician who was not seeing an adequate number of patients per day, and paid insufficient attention to the efficient operation of the practice. On the plus side, they had a loyal patient base and were usually seen by their communities as providing an important service.

Perhaps as a result of the less-than-successful experience with small primary care practices, UHSC next acquired a much larger practice—Anderson Clinic. The large patient volume, lucrative payer mix, and busy physicians have made Anderson Clinic a financial success for UHSC. However, there have been substantial problems with this acquisition as well. Most important, changing the culture of a large practice has been difficult. Most Anderson Clinic physicians have been with the practice a long time and resisted many of the clinical and customer processes introduced by UHSC. Many implementation problems have occurred, and complaints from many physicians have required a lot of UHSC management time. One UHSC manager said, "Anderson gives us most of our profit, but it also gives us most of our headaches."

This less-than-successful experience with small primary care practices and a large practice prompted UHSC to review its practice acquisition strategy. After several months of study, UHSC decided that, although an acquisition can help to reduce practice costs and increase efficiency, the revenue side of the practice is most important. Thus, UHSC has established five criteria for evaluating the acquisition of a practice:

1. Adequate patient volume for the number of providers
2. Viable payer mix
3. Physician productivity
4. Effective operations, including revenue cycle management, pricing of services, coding and documentation, and service mix
5. Qualitative factors, including patient referrals from customer service, organizational culture, quality improvement, and community relations

These criteria have resulted in UHSC adopting a strategy of acquiring "not-too-big and not-too-small" primary care practices. These multiphysician practices are not as financially lucrative as larger practices such as the Anderson Clinic, but incorporation of the practices into the organization has been much easier. Thus, management has decided that this type of practice works best for UHSC and has been looking to acquire more practices of this type.

In the Bedford region of central California, UHSC has acquired several practices in the southern end but does not yet have a practice in the northern end. UHSC practices provide general primary care services only, but UHSC is exploring provision of some specialty services, such as pain clinics. UHSC plans to try some specialty services in a few practices to determine whether there is a business case to support an extensive rollout.

Bedford Clinics

One of the primary care practices that UHSC wants to acquire is Bedford Clinics, which is located in the northern end of the Bedford region. Several years ago, UHSC had targeted Bedford Clinics for acquisition but attempts to interest the two founding partners had failed. At the time, the founders had no interest in being purchased by a larger organization.

Nevertheless, Bedford Clinics was too inviting a takeover target to be overlooked for long. UHSC believes that acquisition of the practice would attract and retain new patients for the network, increase referrals to other UHSC services, and better prepare UHSC for new value-based payment models. Bedford would benefit from access to a larger network and greater net revenue from the UHSC expertise in boosting physician productivity. In addition, some UHSC senior managers know the two Bedford Clinics founders, having served on various community committees together. "The Bedford docs see things the way we see them," a UHSC senior manager recently said. For these reasons, UHSC has continued to follow the physicians and business activities of Bedford Clinics.

Today, Bedford Clinics operates two walk-in facilities and consists of five physicians—three are board certified in family practice and two in internal medicine. Three work full-time and two work part-time, resulting in four full-time equivalent (FTE) physicians. Bedford Clinics is organized as a for-profit corporation, but for tax purposes the business is classified as an S corporation. (In an S corporation, the business pays no taxes. Rather, the corporation's taxable income is constructively distributed to the owners, who pay personal taxes on the income.)

Bedford Clinics was founded 10 years ago by two physicians (the part-timers) who wanted to have more free time than their solo practices allowed. Initially, Bedford Clinics had only one location, but a second was recently added. The downtown clinic is open between 8 a.m. and 2 p.m. and its patients predominantly come directly from work sites. The midtown clinic is open between 8 a.m. and 8 p.m. and its patients mostly come from home; it also provides a few specialty services, including a diabetes care service. Both downtown and midtown clinics are open Monday to Friday, 50 weeks per year. Exhibit 33.1 provides the average number of visits by day for each clinic, and exhibit 33.2 shows the current payer mix. With the current medical and clerical staffs, as well as clinic space, Bedford Clinics' patient volume can grow as much as 50 percent without the need for additional personnel or facilities.

The five physicians who make up Bedford Clinics own the business. However, the two founding partners control the business: Each has a 35 percent ownership stake. The remaining three partners each own 10 percent of the business. Because the founding partners are looking to fully retire in the near future, they would like to sell the business. The remaining partners are less enthusiastic about selling out, but as minority owners their alternatives are limited.

The most recent income statement of the business is provided in exhibit 33.3. Note that the statement uses the effective average tax rate applicable if Bedford Clinics were to file as a C corporation. A condensed balance sheet is contained in exhibit 33.4. If UHSC acquires Bedford Clinics, it would maintain the current debt ratio into the foreseeable future and has an agreement with a lending institution to borrow funds at a rate of 6 percent. In addition to assets used in the day-to-day operations of the business, Bedford Clinics holds nonoperating assets (marketable securities and investment properties). The marketable securities represent a rainy-day fund, and the investment properties were acquired to diversify the asset holdings and revenue stream of Bedford Clinics.

Bedford Clinics's cost structure, listed in exhibit 33.4, is expected to hold in the immediate future, with fixed costs (including depreciation) increasing at a 2 percent annual rate. Furthermore, Bedford Clinics would have to invest roughly $25,000 each year (in Year 1 dollars) in new equipment. Inflation is expected to increase these capital investment amounts by 2 percent per year.

Wilde and Sullivan

To ensure that it did not overpay for a primary care practice again, UHSC retained the services of Wilde and Sullivan, a California firm that specializes in physician practice valuation and appraisal. Heidi Wilde, the managing partner, had recently valued four practices in the central California region, so she decided to use this experience as a starting point in estimating the value of Bedford Clinics to UHSC. Selected data for these acquisitions are shown in exhibit 33.5.

First, Heidi estimated the expected revenue growth rate for the short term (Years 1–5) and the long term (Years 6 and beyond). In reviewing the data in exhibit 33.5, Heidi noted that Bedford Clinics and all the recent practice acquisitions are located in the same geographic area, so it is reasonable to assume that Bedford Clinics faces the same estimated long-term (Years 6 and beyond) revenue growth rate of 2 percent. However, Heidi has found that the short-term (Years 1–5) revenue growth rate of a particular practice depends on the current level of physician productivity: Clinics with relatively low physician productivity have higher short-term (Years 1–5) revenue growth rates because of room for productivity increases. Heidi also believes that there is an opportunity for improved coding and documentation, better revenue cycle management, and an updated chargemaster at Bedford Clinics.

Next, Heidi assembled the information required for the discounted cash flow (DCF) approach, including the estimated required rate of return on an equity investment in Bedford Clinics. Little market data about primary care practices are available to offer guidance, but the current yield on long-term Treasury bonds is 4 percent, and the historical risk premium on the market, which reflects the premium on an average-risk common stock investment, is about 5 percent. Of course, significant risk and liquidity differences exist between direct ownership of a relatively small group practice and ownership of the stock of a large, publicly traded corporation. UHSC also informed Heidi that it estimates its tax rate will be 20 percent for the foreseeable future.

In addition to the DCF approach, Wilde and Sullivan use three market multiple methods to value medical practices: physician FTEs, net patient revenue, and EBITDA (earnings before interest, taxes, depreciation, and amortization). In these methods, a proxy for value is multiplied by a market-determined factor that best expresses the relationship of that proxy to equity value.

With this information, Heidi started the task of estimating the value of Bedford Clinics to UHSC and making a recommendation on whether UHSC should make the acquisition.

EXHIBIT 33.1
Bedford Clinics: Current Average Number of Visits by Day and Clinic

	Downtown	*Midtown*
Monday	42	64
Tuesday	38	53
Wednesday	36	50
Thursday	37	51
Friday	36	37
Total	189	255

EXHIBIT 33.2
Bedford Clinics: Current Payer Mix

Medicaid	9%
Medicare	21%
Private insurance	52%
Out-of-pocket	18%
Total	100%

EXHIBIT 33.3
Bedford Clinics: Current Free Cash Flow Statement

Net revenues	$1,491,791
Operating expenses	
Fixed	719,997
Variable	349,079
Total operating expenses	1,069,076
EBIT	$ 422,715
Interest expense	25,575
EBT	$ 397,140
Taxes	119,142
Net profit	$ 277,998

EBIT: earnings before interest and taxes; EBT: earnings before taxes

Notes: 1. Operating expenses include depreciation of $11,070.
2. Capital expenditures for the year were $15,000.

EXHIBIT 33.4
Bedford Clinics: Current Balance Sheet

Assets	
Cash and cash equivalents	$ 73,475
Marketable securities	42,399
Accounts receivable	85,702
Medical and administrative supplies	9,890
Current assets	$ 211,466
Net plant and equipment	1,689,524
Investment properties	450,461
Total assets	$2,351,451
Liabilities and Owner's Equity	
Notes payable	$ 352,718
Owner's equity	1,998,733
Total liabilities and equity	$2,351,451

Note: Adjustments to the amount of debt in the capital structure occur at year-end. Thus, interest expense on the income statement can be calculated from the previous year's balance of notes payable.

EXHIBIT 33.5
Wilde and Sullivan: Selected Data for Recent Acquisitions of Primary Care Practices in the Bedford Region

	Alvarez Family Health	*Johnson Walk-In Center*	*South Side Clinic*	*Wilson Internal Medicine*
Patient visits	5,600	34,000	40,000	170,000
Net patient revenue	$380,000	$2,400,000	$2,700,000	$13,000,000
EBIT	$159,000	$520,000	$600,000	$2,000,000
Depreciation	$20,000	$80,000	$90,000	$800,000
Full-time physicians	1	2	4	20
Part-time physicians	0	6	3	4
Estimated Years 1–5 revenue growth rate	5%	4%	3%	2%
Price	$800,000	$6,000,000	$7,000,000	$44,000,000

EBIT: earnings before interest and taxes

ABOUT THE AUTHORS

George H. Pink, PhD, is the Humana Distinguished Professor in the Department of Health Policy and Management of the Gillings School of Global Public Health and a senior research fellow at the Cecil G. Sheps Center for Health Services Research at the University of North Carolina at Chapel Hill. Prior to receiving a doctorate in corporate finance, he spent 10 years in health services management, planning, and consulting. Dr. Pink teaches courses in healthcare finance and is involved in several large research projects, including studies of rural hospital financial performance. Over the past 30 years, he has served on the boards and committees of more than 100 hospitals and other healthcare organizations, written more than 90 peer-reviewed articles, and made more than 250 presentations in 10 countries.

Paula H. Song, PhD, is the Richard M. Bracken Chair and Professor in the Department of Health Administration in the College of Health Professions at Virginia Commonwealth University. Her research and teaching interests cover areas such as healthcare financial management, investment strategies in not-for-profit hospitals, payment reform, and business case evaluation for health initiatives. Dr. Song received a doctorate in health services organization and policy as well as master's degrees in health services administration and applied economics from the University of Michigan in Ann Arbor. She has published more than 50 peer-reviewed articles and has coauthored five leading textbooks on healthcare finance. In 2020, she was awarded the John D. Thompson Prize by the Association of University Programs in Health Administration.